THE VENERABLE
F. LOUIS DE PONTE, S.J.

THE LIFE OF
THE VENERABLE
F. LOUIS DE PONTE
of the Society of Jesus

Mediatrix Press
MMXXII

ISBN: 978-1-957066-16-5

The Life of the Venerable Louis de Ponte of the Society of Jesus was originally published by Thomas Richardson and Son, and Derby, London, 1892.

The Mediatrix Press edition has been reprinted and edited in fidelity to the original, changing only British spellings and archaic words. The edits and typography of this edition are ©Mediatrix Press, all rights reserved. No part of this work may be reproduced in physical or electronic format except for quotations for review in journals, blogs, without the express permission of the publisher. No part of this edition may be placed on archive.org.

Mediatrix Press
607 E 6th Ave.
Post Falls, ID 83854
www.mediatrixpress.com

CONTENTS

CHAPTER I
His birth, education, studies, and mode of life, until his entrance into the Society of Jesus. . . 1

CHAPTER II
Fervor of his noviciate. Concludes his course of studies. Is ordained priest. 11

CHAPTER III
His scholastic employments. His solemn profession. 23

CHAPTER IV
He is appointed to govern. With what perfection to himself, and spiritual advantage to his subjects. 33

CHAPTER V
He Resigns the Rectorship. Is Appointed Inspector. Serves the Plague-stricken. 47

CHAPTER VI
He is appointed prefect of the spiritual exercises, to the great advantage of the whole province. 53

CHAPTER VII
His success in the confessional. His esteem of that function. His skill in the direction of souls. 61

CHAPTER VIII
His talent for preaching and giving the spiritual exercises. His care in performing every action perfectly. 75

CHAPTER IX
Some Account of His Writings, and of the Great Good Effected by Them. 81

CHAPTER X
His ardent love of God, and desire to suffer for him. 87

CHAPTER XI
His charity towards his neighbor. 95

CHAPTER XII
Of his lively faith and constant hope in God.
. . . . 101

CHAPTER XIII
Of his profound humility, and other virtues depending upon it. 109

CHAPTER XIV
His mortification and corporal austerities. . . 117

CHAPTER XV
His great purity of soul and body. 127

CHAPTER XVI
His prayer and sublime contemplation. 131

CHAPTER XVII
:   *His obedience and zeal in the observance of his institute.* 139

CHAPTER XVIII
:   *Of his devotion to the Blessed Eucharist.* ... 143

CHAPTER XIX
:   *His tender devotion to our Blessed Lady, his angel-guardian, and to the saints.* 149

CHAPTER XX
:   *Of the supernatural gifts of counsel and discernment of spirits, conferred by God on Father de Ponte, and of his great talent in the direction of souls.* 155

CHAPTER XXI
:   *Prophecies of Father de Ponte, and other gifts conferred on him by God.* 165

CHAPTER XXII
:   *His holy death, and its attendant circumstances* 177

CHAPTER XXIII
:   *Miracles performed by God through the merits of his servant, after his death.* 187

CHAPTER XXIV
:   *Profitable maxims found amongst the writings of Father de Ponte.* 195

To Our Crucified Lord that all glory may be given to His most Holy Name, and to His holy priests, Msgr. Eugene Morris and Fr. Sam Conedera S.J., that the abundant graces of the Immaculate Virgin Mary and the loving presence of Venerable Louis De Ponte S.J. may be with them in both this life and life-everlasting.
In Corde Mariae.

A. M. D. G.

THE LIFE OF
THE VENERABLE
F. LOUIS DE PONTE, S.J.

CHAPTER I

His birth, education, studies, and mode of life, until his entrance into the Society of Jesus.

THE Venerable Father Louis de Ponte was by birth a Spaniard, a great example, and master of Christian perfection, and in the science of mystical theology one of the most celebrated doctors of his age. His family was originally of Biscay, and yielded to none, either in nobility of blood or splendour of connection. He was born at Valladolid, the capital of Old Castile, on the 11th of November, 1554, under the pontificate of Julius III when the Emperor Charles V reigned over the Spanish dominions, and S. Ignatius Loyola governed the Society of Jesus.

His father's name was Alfonso de Ponte, and his mother's Maria Yasquez. They were Christians of the old stamp, and of unblemished probity. As issue of their holy marriage, they had three sons and one daughter, and were so anxious to guard and educate them well, that, in the general opinion, their house resembled a religious noviciate. Donna Anna, the daughter, was the first-born. In due time she assumed the habit of the glorious Saint Dominic, and was such a perfect religious, that it is said and believed that after her death God revealed to one of His chosen souls the glory which she enjoyed in heaven. Of the sons, Louis was the eldest. Andrew and John, like their sister, embraced the institute of the same most holy patriarch, in which both progressed so happily as to be numbered amongst the illustrious men of an order so justly renowned. Andrew was a religious of consummate perfection, of great union with God, most zealous for the salvation of souls, and was for a long time employed by his superiors in the important office of master of novices. John, having taken his degree as master, was qualificator of the holy inquisition, and historian to their Catholic majesties, and both in government employment, and in the professor's chair, gave brilliant proofs of his ability.

Louis was but a mere youth when death deprived him of his father. He remained under his mother's care, a matron of equal piety and prudence. She anxiously devoted herself to the task of grounding him solidly in the holy fear of God, and having him instructed in all those duties which constitute a Christian nobleman, doing this with all the more assiduity, because the hopes of the family centred in Louis, as being the eldest. Nor in this regard had she much difficulty, owing to the docile and ingenuous disposition of the child, and his great maturity of mind.

His singular piety would lead us to infer that, in addition to his mother's care, Almighty God Himself was his immediate Master, preventing him with His celestial benedictions, and admitting him to close intimacy with Himself in prayer. And in effect it was surprising to find him, before he had completed his twelfth year, frequently on his knees, in some remote corner of the house, spending whole hours in sweet converse with our Lord, and receiving new lessons how to love and serve Him better. He arose before dawn, and in his domestic oratory gave full vent to his devotion; and at daybreak, even in the severest winter, always went to assist at the first Mass in the neighbouring church of the Dominicans.

In the same spirit he performed all his other actions of the day, doing everything with such judgment, exactitude, and attention, that more could not have been required from a full-grown man. Whilst on this subject we may cite the words of his brother, Father Andrew, as given upon oath before the ordinary, in the process for the beatification of the servant of God: "Louis from his earliest age began to serve God in truth and with great perfection, never diverting himself by anything that was not virtuous, or that could not serve as an example to others."

From this his intimate communication with God, sprung forth, as from its root, that virginal modesty which checked the greatest boldness; that invincible meekness, notwithstanding his quick, and as we may say, fiery character; that assiduity in ever mortifying his own will; and that ardent desire of advancing continually in the path of perfection; a desire fomented by frequenting the sacraments, by assiduously assisting at sermons, by severity to his own body, and by the daily exercise of an ardent charity towards his neighbour. We may remark here, that when a mere child, it was his pious custom, morning and evening, to visit the sick in the neighbouring hospital, serving them in every way, and suggesting pious thoughts to them, to the great admiration of those who witnessed it.

The continual exercise of so many virtues together did not, however, in the least withdraw him from full application to his studies at their appointed time. Being convinced that learning assists us the better to know and love God, he divided the hours of the day so that study never interfered with piety, nor was piety any detriment to study. He thus soon mastered grammar and humanities, and went through his course of philosophy in the university of Valladolid, where he was considered to be one of the most brilliant scholars. Having obtained his degree of bachelor, he went to study theology under the Dominican Fathers, in their celebrated convent of Saint Gregory.

It is true that he at the same time frequented the Jesuit schools in the college of S. Ambrose, then recently opened, to hear the theological lectures of the renowned theologian Francis Suarez; and I believe this to have been a special disposition of Divine Providence, that by means of so great a man, no less holy than learned, Louis might become acquainted with the Society, of which he had hitherto known little or nothing. The youth was charmed with the religious virtue and the affable manners of Suarez; he began to examine more minutely the order to which he belonged, —its laws, maxims, and the economy of its government.

He had reached the nineteenth year of his age when Father Martin Guttierez was sent to Valladolid,

EARLY LIFE

to be superior of the professed house there. This Martin Guttierez was a man filled with the spirit of God, most dear to his divine Mother, who honored him with several visits, a most zealous preacher, and successful in the conversion of many souls. At the death of S. Francis Borgia, he was sent by his province to Rome, to assist at the election of a new general. Passing through France, he fell into the hands of the Huguenots, who, in hatred of Catholicity, imprisoned him, where, overwhelmed with labors, he passed to a glorious life. No sooner had Guttierez entered upon his new office, than he became famous in the pulpit, where it was one and the same thing to hear him, and to find the people excited to such compunction as only to think of settling their accounts with God, and doing penance for their sins. Louis was one of his most assiduous hearers, and assuredly was not amongst the number of those who were least affected by the discourses of the zealous preacher.

Up to this time he had had no other aim in all his actions than to sanctify himself and become pleasing to God, without, however, forming any determination with regard to a state of life. The preaching of Guttierez enlightened and taught him still better the insufficiency and vanity of all human things. He felt himself impelled to abandon the world, and assume the habit of the society; neither did he feel any great repugnance to retire into a cloister, having already occasionally experienced the wish. But as for embracing the Institute of S. Ignatius, he certainly did feel a strong repugnance to do so. Although he had conceived an esteem of it, it was in fact but a new order; and seeing it hated and persecuted everywhere, he felt unwilling to join it. Besides, in the event of his choosing the religious state, his inclination led him to the order of S. Dominic, which was ancient and creditable, from whence, too, he had first imbibed the milk of piety and letters.

Notwithstanding all his repugnances, never did he hear Guttierez without feeling himself drawn, as it were, by the hand to the society; so much so, that it seemed to him that an angel, not a man, addressed him by the mouth of the preacher. It would be difficult to describe the internal conflict he underwent, without knowing how to decide. In this uncertainty he prolonged his prayers, and macerated himself with severe austerities, in order to understand more clearly from God what was His divine will. But our loving Lord did not deign to console him so soon. Instead of being calmed his uneasiness increased; especially as at that very time obedience called Guttierez elsewhere, so that he knew not whom to consult. However, the tender heart of his good God could not keep him longer in suspense, and He began, as we may say, to make known His will on the following occasion. Up to this time Louis had always clung to the pious opinion in favor of the Immaculate Conception of our Blessed Lady, a belief most gratifying to her, and highly to her honor. Now, in a public disputation he happened one day to hear the opinion contested. I know not why, but he changed his own, and declared for the opposite side. The change cost him dearly, for at that same moment the vein of devotion in his soul was dried up; no more celestial consolations, no more of the sweets of paradise, no more good thoughts, no more sweet affections for God. On the contrary, when disposing himself for prayer, he felt a nausea, and was disgusted with every pious duty, until he thought heaven was shut against him, and that Almighty God had abandoned him. Such an unexpected change, all the more painful as being so little apprehended, threw the afflicted youth into great consternation, nor could he discover its cause. He examined himself minutely, sought counsel from others, but all in vain. At length he began to suspect that it might be a chastisement from our Blessed Lady for his infidelity in renouncing the pious opinion, as above narrated. He resumed it that very moment, obliging himself by vow never to relinquish it again. He had guessed the truth; no sooner had he made his vow than our Lord turned to console him, and looked on him with the same favorable eye as heretofore.

But though, as everyone will see, this vow bound the heart of Louis, it did not so bind his tongue as to prevent him from arguing in a contrary sense, when merely done by way of scholastic disputation. It so happened that he was invited to this, and consented. However upright the young man's intention may have been, it was not pleasing to the Mother of God, who required that the sacrifice of her servant should be entire; she took care to make him understand this, but did it with the resentment of a mother. On the day appointed for the disputation, no sooner did Louis enter the arena than all the arguments, all the doctrinal reasons prepared for the occasion, entirely escaped his memory. Confounded at so unexpected an event, and equally afflicted, he felt, though late, from whence the blow proceeded. Bathed in tears, he repaired to Mary's altar, and bound himself by another vow, that if she would lead him safely out of this difficulty, he would entirely devote himself, with all his heart, mind, and tongue, to the defense of the doctrine of her Immaculate Conception. Mary was moved to compassion; she restored to his memory all that he had forgotten, and confided to him the necessary arms to combat an opinion, which in his case had been merely feigned.

These two incidents were personal, and the being aware, as he was, that the society considered the pious belief in the Immaculate Conception as peculiarly its own doctrine, gained the heart of Louis to the order, so that, in spite of all his repugnance, he determined to embrace it. This generous resolution calmed all his uneasiness, and he only waited for a convenient opportunity to put it in execution.

His peace, however, was but of short duration. The devil even then foresaw the losses he should afterwards sustain at the hands of such a man, especially when sequestered from the world, and clothed with the habit of religion. He excited in his soul a new tempest, the fiercest he had ever yet sustained, and to which no other had given rise. He suggested the idea, that whichever religious institute he embraced, he would be unhappy for the rest of his life. So many and so great were the hardships and difficulties to be met with at every step, as to be quite insupportable to poor humanity; and this tempest, described by himself in the nineteenth chapter of his "Life of Father Balthazar Alvarez," continued for six months. At length, observing that whenever he was calm in prayer, he always felt it to be the will of God that he should enter the society, he began to discover the deceit of the infernal foe. He consulted his superiors on the subject, and having obtained the necessary permissions, without losing another moment he took the habit, on the second of December, 1574, being twenty years of age, and having completed his second year of theology.

CHAPTER II

Fervour of his noviciate. Concludes his course of studies. Is ordained priest.

LOUIS, being received into the society, was sent by his superiors to Medina del Campo, where the noviciate of the province was situated. No sooner did he find himself within those blessed walls, and witnessed the regularity reigning there, the fervour of so many youths despising all worldly things, the holy alacrity with which each one strove to mortify self, their reciprocal charity in helping one another, their modesty, recollection, and love of prayer, than all this filled him with sincere joy; and with a heart in perfect peace, he never ceased blessing God and His infinite mercy for admitting him to partake of so great a good. Nor from this time forward did the devil ever dare to molest him with a single thought of sorrow or regret for the step he had taken.

As it is the practice of the society that the new postulants, before they join their companions, should for a month go through the Spiritual Exercises of S. Ignatius, thus to detach them from the world, and attach them to religious life, Louis entered upon this school of perfection with a "great and generous soul," as our holy founder requires. We could not easily describe the fervour with which he gave himself to the consideration of the eternal truths, and the mysteries of our redemption, nor the lively desires he conceived of giving himself entirely to God, and of being a true imitator of Jesus Christ, following the traces of His most holy and divine examples.

With such firm resolutions as these did he conclude the exercises, and enter upon his noviciate career. His principal study was at once to give himself to a familiar and continual communication with God, spending with Him all the time free from other common duties; and as it would be useless to heat the iron in the furnace, unless we reduced it to the form intended with strokes of the hammer, so he chose prayer as the most likely means to acquire mortification, vigilantly watching over himself, and subduing every depraved inclination, insomuch that he, who was naturally choleric, became in a very short time one of the meekest of men, to the great astonishment of everybody.

Not content with opening his whole heart, and disclosing every interior movement to his superior, in whom he considered the person of Jesus Christ Himself, he publicly accused himself of his defects, and fearful of not knowing them sufficiently, on his knees he would implore others to admonish him of them with full liberty. No one could be more humble than he was; he put himself beneath the feet of all, looking upon everyone as better than himself. He was always the first in the most lowly and laborious offices, such as carrying wood or water, serving the

NOVITIATE AND ORDINATION

cook, and other similar things. That he might triumph over all human respects, and bid defiance to the world, of which so many are the willing slaves, he, with permission of the superiors, would put on an old habit of another color, as if he were the foot-boy or a day laborer, and thus accompany the purveyor to the market or public square, and there loading his shoulders with a large basket of vegetables, fruit, or meat, he would carry it home in the sight of everyone.

From time to time he was sent to serve the sick in the hospital, where there was no office of charity, how abject soever it might be, that he would not undertake, even carrying with his own hands the most repulsive vessels to the neighboring stream, there to wash them. One day he found in some corner of the hospital a miserable object, covered with wounds from head to foot, and almost forsaken by everyone, on account of the horrible stench issuing from him. Louis' heart was moved with the deepest compassion, and procuring a clean shirt and some linen from the person who had the charge of these things, he began with great satisfaction to remove the filth in which this half putrid creature seemed almost buried, and so thoroughly cleansed him, that without exaggeration we may say he restored him to new life. This act was so agreeable to God, that in recompense he, as many remarked, received some striking advantages in the way of perfection.

With equal diligence he undertook to subdue his body, and prevent its waging war against the spirit, by rigorous fasts, severe flagellations, rough hair shirts; and all the watchfulness and authority of superiors were requisite to curb his excessive ardor. On festivals he went out into the public places to teach children the Christian doctrine, to their great advantage, and to the great edification of those who witnessed it. Louis was in his second year of noviciate, when his superiors, convinced of his spiritual proficiency and solid virtue, thought proper to send him to Valladolid, to finish his course of studies, even before the expiration of the term of noviciate, towards the end of March, 1576. He obeyed with the utmost promptitude, though not without an inward regret, both because he was leaving a house which to him had seemed like paradise, and because he should again find himself in the midst of his relatives, whom he had already entirely relinquished, except to recommend them to God. This proximity only tended to place his heroic virtue in a clearer light, and prove his utter detachment from the ties of flesh and blood. Arrived in the city, he did not vouchsafe his family a single visit. His superior, though much edified by his religious comportment on the one hand, thought, however, that duty required him to pay his respects to his mother, and gave him an order to that effect; but such was his modesty, that on entering her house he fixed his eyes upon the ground, not venturing to raise them to look at her, nor did he speak a word. His prudent mother, so far from being offended, loved him better than ever, and venerated him as a Saint. This same spirit of generous detachment continued during the many years he remained in that city.

On arriving at Valladolid, Louis, by the permission of God, was assigned a room exposed to the north wind, in fact, the coldest room in the college, in which he had much to suffer, and being of rather a delicate constitution, and particularly susceptible of cold, he frequently became quite stiff, and unable to move. Yet he never uttered a word of complaint, submitting with great content, because it was close to the chapel, and he could retire to pray before an image of our Blessed Lady whenever he had time at his own disposal.

He resumed his theological studies with all the more pleasure because he again had for master the most learned and renowned Francis Suarez, of whose sanctity and learning he had the highest opinion. He soon gave fresh proofs of the depth and acuteness of his intellect in proof of which it will suffice to say that Suarez himself often conferred with him on the most difficult questions then in vogue, not as a master with a scholar, but as one master would with another, declaring that he was much assisted by the lights he received from the young man.

Although he studied with all his application, nevertheless, such was his inward recollection and union with God, such his external comportment, such his exact observance of the least rule, such, in fine, the rigor of his private and public penances, that in the opinion of everyone in the college he perfectly fulfilled the duties of a diligent scholastic and a fervent novice. And because he could not at this time spend as much time in prayer as he could wish, and as he had done at Medina, he made a compact with his own heart not to allow any moment to pass without offering to God the tribute of some good act. Even when walking, he was so lost in God as not to notice what passed around him.

Not being allowed to serve the cook, or employ himself in other abject offices, his humility and charity could not remain idle; therefore, at certain times he assisted the infirmarian, sweeping the rooms, arranging the beds, and performing any other service for the sick that lay in his power. If any invalid needed more than ordinary assistance, he would beg on his knees, as a great favor, to have charge of him, promising to use the utmost care. During the vacation, having obtained the superior's leave, he undertook the office of infirmarian, often laborious enough, and discharged it with as much punctuality, attention, and relish, as if it had been a mere recreation to him. It is not easy to describe the Fervor he enkindled in those who were in health, or the solace and comfort he afforded the sick, on finding themselves assisted with so much charity by this angel in human form.

His two years of noviciate being completed, added to the fervent preparation which might be expected from him, it was with indescribable consolation of soul that he realized his ardent desire of consecrating himself entirely to God by the vows of religion, which ceremony took place in the college of S. Ambrose, on the feast of the Immaculate Conception. This new tie bound him still more closely to his good God, and was another powerful incentive to love Him still more perfectly, and to undertake great things for His glory.

About this time the procurator of Japan came over in search of recruits for the missions of that vast empire. Louis felt an ardent desire to be one of the number chosen to convey the light of the Gospel to those blind Gentiles, being ready to shed his blood and give his life for Jesus Christ. Frequent and urgent were his entreaties to this effect; but our Lord, who destined him to a longer and not less painful martyrdom,

NOVITIATE AND ORDINATION 17

satisfied with his good-will, would not permit the execution of it. This only served to render the holy young man still more humble, and he protested that his sins made him unworthy of such an honor. Having concluded his course of studies, and being in the twenty-fourth year of his age, he and some other companions were sent to the college at Ognate, founded by S. Francis Borgia about twenty- seven years before. The sweet and ever fresh recollection of the examples of heroic virtue left by the holy duke, who had there put on the habit of the society, was not lost on Louis; it served as a spur to urge him in the path of perfection; he strove to imitate him as far as possible, especially in his profound humility, mortification, and contempt of the world. He continued here till October, 1579, when he was sent to Villa- Garcia, to go through the last trial prescribed by our holy founder for those who embrace his society, intended, as we may say, to repair the strength of soul, enervated by study, and to provide a new stock of Fervor whereby to exercise our ministry with greater efficacy.

In Villa-Garcia he had the good fortune to have for master and director of his conscience Father Baltazar Alvarez, universally esteemed as a man of eminent sanctity and sublime contemplation, of whom we presume the reader will not be displeased to hear S. Teresa's opinion. He was her director for some years, and we can judge from her writings how dear he was to her as a master, and how much she profited by his instruction. When speaking of Father Alvarez, this great Saint said, amongst other things: "He is the person to whom in this life my soul is the most indebted." Once, when assisting at his Mass, she saw his head crowned with brilliant rays of light. On another occasion she asserted that our Lord had revealed to her that he was of the number of the predestinated, and had shown her at the same time the high seat of glory reserved for him in heaven, giving her to understand, moreover, that he had reached to such a degree of perfection as to be surpassed by no one then on earth. Finally, when the blessed woman heard of his death, she wept bitterly for more than an hour. When asked the subject of her tears, she replied, "I weep because I know what a loss the Church of God will suffer by the death of this His servant."

No sooner did Louis appear to give an account of himself to his superior, Father Baltazar, in whom he beheld the person of Jesus Christ, than, with the greatest humility, but at the same time with full openness of heart, he sincerely manifested his conscience, concealing nothing, in order that he might have an intimate and entire knowledge of him. Father Alvarez listened to him in silence, with his eyes immovably fixed on a crucifix, and by way of answer only gave him these few precise words: "This virtue is altogether puerile, nevertheless it is necessary to cultivate and strengthen it."

No doubt this great master of spirit saw at once how great a soul God had given him to cultivate in the person of this young man. No sooner did he perceive how far advanced Louis was in the ways of God, than he admired his ardent desires to become a saint, his love of prayer, his resolute will to mortify and contradict himself and his self-love in everything; so

NOVITIATE AND ORDINATION 19

that we may presume that when he called his virtue puerile, he intended it as a stimulus to prevent his stopping on the road, whilst there still remained so much to be done before arriving at perfection. The event proved the correctness of the idea. The answer of the superior produced two admirable effects in the soul of the good youth; one was to make him humble himself profoundly before God, acknowledging that he was but a mere beginner in the school of virtue, needing also much study and much help; the other was to confirm a determined resolution to use his utmost endeavors, cost what it might, to perfect himself and to belong entirely to God.

Neither did Louis for a moment defer putting his hand to the work, by reducing his good resolutions to practice, by a more assiduous application to prayer, a more attentive watchfulness over himself and his own heart, in order to eradicate every affection that was not for God. To obtain this the more easily, he most earnestly besought Almighty God to give him such a practical knowledge as should undeceive his mind, and at the same time invigorate his will, to understand and love only whatever was most pleasing to Him. Our good Lord did not refuse him this consolation, and signified to him, as a safeguard against error, that his chief study was to be the acquisition of humility and obedience.

One of the rewards of his pious desires was our Lord's beginning to deal more familiarly with him, speaking interiorly to him, as He is accustomed to do with chosen souls, thus to make him understand His divine will. The young man being timid, and unskilled in this language, was doubtful whether the voice proceeded from the good or the evil spirit. Our Lord Himself asked him this question, "What wouldst thou do if someone offered thee a branch laden with fruit?" to which he answered, "I would eat the fruit, and throw away the branch." "And that is what thou oughtest to do," rejoined Almighty God. "Do the good works suggested to thee. If they be such and likely to promote thy spiritual profit, do not trouble thyself to ascertain by what voice they are proposed."

Father Alvarez did not fail to cultivate a soil so well disposed. He daily gave Louis new and more sublime lessons of spirituality, trying him at the same time with various kinds of humiliation. From time to time he sent him to Rio-Secco, a small town about three leagues from Villa- Garcia, on foot, dressed in a coarse cassock of another color, to accompany the purveyor to the market, where of course there was a large concourse of people, and to carry home on his shoulders the provisions purchased for the house. At other times he would send him with one of the novices into the neighboring villages to preach to the country people, and teach them the Christian doctrine. Then again he would send him, with other priests his companions, to give little missions in various places. He obeyed in all these things with such promptitude and cheerfulness as to give great edification, and produced such fruit as to astonish even the master himself. Although in the house Louis conversed indifferently with all, he preferred the society of those whom he knew to be the more perfect, endeavoring to copy in himself whatever he saw good in each one. His conversation was always of God or of holy things connected with his own advancement. He most

NOVITIATE AND ORDINATION

frequently, and as often as he was permitted, discoursed with his beloved Father Alvarez, from whom, according to his own remark, he never departed without a lesson on one or other of the virtues. He most relished those exhortations given by the holy master on the rules of the institute, and that he might not lose the remembrance or advantage of them, he made an exact compendium of them, of which several copies were taken, and being distributed, contributed much to promote a stricter observance of the said rules.

Towards the end of the year 1579, Louis received the order of subdeacon, and the following year was made deacon. When he had completed his twenty-fifth year, his superiors informed him that he was to be ordained priest. The humble young man was at first terrified at the idea of assuming a character formidable even to the angels, though at the same time no news could have given him greater comfort and consolation, under the happy hope that in this furnace of charity he should be wholly transformed into God. To prepare himself with the greatest possible application, he made the Spiritual Exercises, fully resolved wholly to despoil himself of the old man, and put on the new. It was fortunate for him that Father Alvarez made his retreat precisely at the same time, having just been appointed to the provincialship of Toledo. In this blessed solitude Louis had no dealings except with God and his holy director, who, in endeavoring to perfect him, disclosed the wonderful treasures which his loving Lord had bestowed on his own soul. The subjects most frequently discussed were the poverty, sufferings, and humiliations of Jesus

Christ, the three inseparable companions of His holy life, and which must also be our companions, if we aim at resemblance with Him, in which all our happiness consists.

Having concluded the exercises, Louis was resolved to do great things for God. He shed tears of tender affection on being separated from his beloved Father Alvarez, to whom he declared himself indebted for whatever there was good in his soul, and started for Valladolid, where he was ordained priest on the festival of S. Joseph, the 19th of March, and said his first Mass on the Annunciation. Being ordained priest, and empowered to hear confessions, his superiors appointed him to that function, Holy Week and Easter being at hand. He continued it until called elsewhere.

CHAPTER III

His scholastic employments. His solemn profession.

FATHER LOUIS was for several years engaged in scholastic employments, to the great advantage of his province, and of those persons whose good fortune it was to have him for their master. No sooner was he made priest than his superiors sent him to Salamanca, that he might defend theology in that celebrated university, no longer in quality of scholar, but of master; a very rare honor indeed, conferred only on a few others similar to himself. In this office he gave such proofs of talent, wisdom, and erudition, joined to such great humility and modesty, as excited the astonishment and admiration of all who heard him.

He acquired an equally high reputation for sanctity both within and without the college during the few months he remained there; ever foremost in all regular duties, spending much time in prayer before the most Blessed Sacrament, cherishing silence and interior union with God, assisting everyone with an insatiable charity, even in the most abject offices, deeming himself the last and lowest in the house, gaining everyone by his sweetness, meekness, and other virtues.

At the beginning of the year 1581 he was appointed professor of philosophy at Leon, a chair of high reputation. In this new employment he prescribed for himself these two laws: the first was a continual watchfulness over himself and all his actions, that study might not cool his ardor in the acquisition of perfection; the second was, never to spare his own fatigue and labor in the advancement of the scholars committed to him, either in piety or learning, being accustomed to say that it was the duty of religious masters to do all they could to promote Christian virtues in their pupils, otherwise the issue of their teaching would be miserable indeed. With these maxims firmly rooted in his mind and heart, it is inconceivable with what diligence he prepared his writings; his matter was so lucid, clear, and well arranged, that, however difficult the subject might be, it became intelligible even to the dullest intellect. Nor was he content with explaining it once or twice; he illustrated it by examples and similitudes so appropriate and easy, that it was almost impossible not to understand them. Everyone had full liberty to apply to him at any hour, to propose their doubts and queries, sure of always finding him most ready to receive and satisfy them, with an affability and charity that gained all hearts.

At the same time he allowed no lesson to pass without seasoning it with some salutary instruction for the good of souls, inculcating now one, now another of the eternal truths, and the necessity of living in the holy fear of God prescribing sometimes to

SOLEMN PROFESSION

all in common, sometimes to each one in particular, the best means of avoiding those dangers to which youth is most exposed. Seldom did it happen that the scholars left his classes without compunction, and without being animated to lead lives worthy of Christians.

If he so zealously endeavored to sanctify externs, he was still more assiduous with regard to the Jesuit students. Besides the efficacy of his most holy and admirable example, being always amongst them in every exercise of piety and mortification, he very frequently called them privately to his room, under the pretext of advancing them in philosophy and clearing its obscurities, taking advantage of these opportunities to discourse on spiritual things, and instruct them in the best means of acquiring virtue, doing this with such affability, charity, and discretion, that they loved him not only as a master, but as a father, and each one sedulously strove to imitate his example as well as follow his counsels.

With regard to the sanctification of his own soul, it may be said that in a very short time he filled the whole college with the odor of his virtues, nor was it long ere it became diffused throughout the city, in consequence of which great numbers, especially of the nobility, begged him to become their constant director. Although his humility led him to prefer the direction of the poor, he knew not how to refuse himself to anyone. Besides his natural talent for the direction of souls, which he so well led on to virtue, God had conferred on him a special gift in this respect; and, in fact, a sensible change of life was soon observed in most of his penitents, and numerous were the conversions he effected. Amongst many others was a nobleman of the highest rank in Spain, who, touched by the holy instructions of the servant of God, changed his conduct, applying himself seriously to the salvation of his soul. By an almost continual prayer, severe penances, and abundant alms, he disposed himself to spend holily the short remnant of his life. In the meantime Almighty God was pleased to give him an anticipated knowledge of his death, either immediately to himself, or more probably by means of his director. The nobleman was by no means alarmed at the announcement; on the contrary, he with a cheerful countenance informed his family on several different occasions that he should shortly die. At first, when his wife and children heard him say this, they only laughed, seeing him not only in good, but even in robust health. However, as he persisted in his assertion, they, ascribing it to hypochondria, endeavored to divert his mind, and engaged him to share in a party of pleasure which was publicly to take place in the city. But before the day appointed for the festivity arrived, the nobleman fell dangerously ill. He immediately summoned Father de Ponte, made his confession, received the last rites of the Church and, with the servant of God still at his side, died, overflowing with consolation.

On Sundays and festivals, accompanied by some of his scholars, he repaired to one or other of the adjacent villages, where, collecting the people in the church, he preached to them with so much Fervor, and excited their compunction so effectually, that he was obliged to spend several hours in hearing their confessions; nor did all this satisfy them, for they would go on other days to the town on purpose to see him.

Another of his principal occupations was to teach the catechism to little children, adapting himself to their capacity with invincible patience, persuaded as he was that this was one of the most effectual means of benefitting the public. Almighty God did not fail to reward his labors, and the zeal he displayed in the promotion of His glory, opening His hand to enrich the soul of His servant with heavenly blessings and sweetness.

Whilst pursuing this holy manner of life, having sanctified his beloved disciples, he concluded his course of philosophy, and was appointed to read theology at Salamanca, where he at once acquired the reputation of being one of the most celebrated masters of that renowned university; so much so, that great numbers belonging to other schools had recourse to him following his rules and direction in their studies, and consulting him on all the most abstruse points of that divine science. Notwithstanding all the additional labor thus imposed upon him, he would hear them all, and satisfy them with so much modesty and humility as soon to captivate all hearts. This universal benevolence was valuable to him, inasmuch as it enabled him to benefit their souls, giving him the opportunity of suggesting some salutary admonition or instruction, since he took care to allow no such opportunity to pass by unheeded.

His multifarious occupations would not permit him to go into the country on festivals, to exercise the usual apostolic functions, as he had done in Leon. To supply this deficiency, he was most assiduous in the confessional, an immense number of persons having placed their consciences in his hands.

It is true this lasted only for one year, his talents calling him to govern for the greater benefit of the province, as will be seen in the next chapter. But his feeble health would not allow him to bear the weight of government very long; so that, after seven or eight years, or about the year 1593, he was appointed professor, and again gave lectures in theology at Valladolid, being at the same time chief prefect of studies. For the sake of uniformity of subject, I may here interrupt the order of time a little, and give a sketch of his conduct during his scholastic ministry.

In the chair of theology at Valladolid, Father Louis was the same as he had been in Leon and Salamanca, excepting, perhaps, that he even seemed to surpass himself. Such was his reputation, that many were of opinion that his learning was infused, not acquired. Although he had been several years removed from the professor's chair, and distracted by other occupations, there was no point of learning, how knotty soever it might be, that seemed new to him, or that he could not unravel, always possessing the necessary information. Nor was his progress less in sanctity of life than was his reputation for theological learning. Above all, there was no one who did not marvel at seeing such profound humility and modesty allied with such rich natural endowments and sublime gifts. It was owing to this virtue of humility that God so delighted in the soul of Louis, and took such pains to consolidate him in it, sometimes even withdrawing His own divine lights and leaving him to his own resources, to humble him the more. In the year 1595, as he was once explaining the subject of the Holy Eucharist, with that vivacity of mind and depth of learning so peculiar to himself, all at once his ideas became clouded, and a torrent of doubt with regard to this divine mystery sprung up in his heart. He left no means untried to dissipate and expel these thoughts at once. But so great was his uneasiness that he changed color, and almost lost the power of speech. He could not possibly extricate himself, or proceed, to the alarm of the scholars, who thought he was suddenly taken ill. Nothing remained for him but to dismiss the school and withdraw to His own room. What then? He had been there but a few moments when he was called to the church, to a lady whose conscience he directed. It was the celebrated Donna Marina D'Escobar, of whom more will be said later. Entering his confessional, the lady said, "Pardon me, father, if I inconvenience you; perhaps your reverence was engaged on some matter of importance?" "A few moments ago," said he, "while explaining the subject of the Eucharist to my scholars" "Oh! father," the lady interposed, "listen to what occurred to me last night on this mystery. All at once I was assailed with such a storm of doubts upon the subject as scarcely to know where I was." She then explained them one by one, to the great astonishment of her director, for they were precisely the same that had troubled him. "Notwithstanding," continued she, "I ceased not to help myself with such speculations and reasons as quite convinced me; the tempest is now over, and, thanks be to God, I am in perfect peace." "But," inquired the father, "what are your reasons?" As she unfolded them one by one, the cloud was dispelled from his mind, and a new light, as it were, sprung up in his soul. Before Donna Marina had ceased speaking, every doubt had disappeared, and he regained his usual calm. Whereupon Louis eagerly humbled himself before God, thanking Him for having, by means of a simple woman, instructed him so well. Full of confusion, he exclaimed, "I will confess to Thee, Lord! because Thou hast hidden these things from the learned, and hast revealed them to little ones!"

The last scholastic employment discharged, by Father de Ponte for many years was the prefectship of studies in this same college; an office of great honor, and of no less anxiety. With what vigilance and strength of soul he discharged this duty may be inferred from what has been already said. His great care was to have all proceed in good order, without disputes and contention, always useless, and often the cause of serious disturbance. Never would he allow a master to teach any novelty or ill-founded or dangerous doctrine. For this purpose he would himself read over their writings, and if he met with any desultory sentence, would go himself to the master's room, and with the greatest modesty and humility propose what he thought contrary to it, never giving up until he was entirely satisfied. Although habitually infirm, and oppressed with several maladies at once, he assisted at all the examinations, disputations, and other scholastic functions. If he found anyone of poor capacity, less prompt in grasping the argument proposed, it is inconceivable with what charity he helped him. He himself would propose the difficulty with such brevity and clearness, that not to come off with honor, one must indeed have been of obtuse

SOLEMN PROFESSION

mind and cloudy brain. In fine, all went on with so much harmony, that scholars as well as masters, admiring his rectitude, discretion, and prudence, loved him tenderly, and always showed him the utmost respect and deference.

Father General Acquaviva, being informed of the excellent endowments and religious virtue of Father Louis, sent him notice of his solemn profession, received by the servant of God with sentiments of the most tender gratitude and profound humility. To prepare himself the better for this great sacrifice, and to purify the victim which was to be entirely consumed in holocaust to the Divine Majesty, he repaired to Medina, where, by prolonged prayer, rigorous penances, and a more exact research into his own heart and its internal movements, he strove to render himself worthy of the honor which he received on the 24th of January, 1593, at the age of thirty-nine, of which he had spent nineteen years in Religion. He made his solemn profession with acts of the most sublime religious virtues.

CHAPTER IV

He is appointed to govern. With what perfection to himself, and spiritual advantage to his subjects.

FATHER LOUIS had acquitted himself so admirably in the chair as professor, that in a very short time he was held to be one of the greatest theologians then living in Spain. Nevertheless, the brilliant qualifications and religious virtues with which he was so abundantly furnished led his superiors to think it would tend more to the glory of God and the advantage of the society if he were appointed to govern the college of the province.

With this view, towards the end of 1585, he was sent to Villa-Garcia, as companion to Father Jerome Ripalda, then master of novices, as well as rector and guide of those young priests who, according to the intention of S. Ignatius, having completed their course of studies, spend one year in devout exercises, thus to refresh their spiritual strength, weakened by assiduous application to learning, and at the same time to lay in a stock of solid virtue and other well-seasoned armor, with which to wage war against hell.

These fathers are commonly called "Fathers of the Third Year."

Louis remained but a short time in this employment, for a few weeks after his arrival Ripalda was sent elsewhere, and the Father General appointed him to the three offices thus vacated.

When he entered upon his new office, his first maxim of government was to lead the way by his own example, "Factus forma Gregis ex animo." He therefore gave himself up to a stricter communication with God in prayer, spending in it all the time left free from other duties. Most frequent were his visits to our Lord in the Blessed Sacrament, and when unable in the day to satisfy his devotion, he spent a great part of the night, and often the whole night, before it, on his knees, immoveable as if in an ecstasy. Even in exterior actions, such was at all times his internal union with God, that he never lost sight of the divine presence.

To prayer he joined the greatest mortification; he let slip no opportunity of overcoming every movement that deviated in the least, from the straight line of duty. His food was sparing, and his sleep, always taken dressed as he was, and on a bench too narrow to allow a change of position, was still more sparing. Though of very delicate constitution, and habitually suffering from many complaints at once, he never omitted to take every night a long and severe discipline.

A contemner of himself and of the world, he wore an old patched discolored habit, such as is usually given to the novices. He was the first at every regular duty, and although superior, he always considered himself the last in the house, sometimes helping the cook, sometimes attending to the stoves, or scouring the kitchen utensils, sometimes sweeping the rooms, and arranging the beds of the sick. This was his constant mode of life all the years of his government; daily perfecting himself more and more by the non-interrupted exercise of every virtue: from whence we may easily infer what must have been his endeavors to perfect all those committed to his care.

To begin with his novices, those tender plants requiring so much training, —children of a few days old, whose food must be prepared before they can be wholly weaned. There was no tenderness of maternal love that he did not employ towards these his dear sons. Frequently would he call, first one, and then another, and with affection beaming in his eyes, inquire about their health, whether they were satisfied with their vocation, what trials they met with, and whether they were in want of anything. He never met them without a smile and some little friendly useful salutation. Every week he saw each one of them in private; nevertheless, his room was ever open to them all, both day and night. Go when they would, they were sure to find him ready to hear, console, and assist them. But if anyone of them fell ill, O! then it was that his charity surpassed itself; everything was done, he spared no attention, stopped at no expense that might contribute to his recovery, even calling in the assistance of doctors from a distance. Attention to the sick could even withdraw him from prayer, so frequent were his visits to them, striving to let them have no reason to regret the indulgences of a paternal roof. If the complaint, instead of being checked, increased, he spent whole hours with them by day and night, to comfort and animate them, performing even the meanest services for them. It is incredible what comfort his affectionate care imparted to the sick, and how much his holy admonitions cheered them.

It is true his great condescension and charity for their health contributed much to win their hearts, and disposed them the more willingly to accept his instructions for the advantage of their souls. Placing in their hands the rules of the institute, he would say to them, "This is the book containing the compact between yourself and God; study it attentively, and observe it faithfully." He daily made them a fervent exhortation, either on the great favor God conferred on them, by removing them in early life from the dangers of a deceitful world, or on the strict obligation of corresponding with such a grace. How good and joyful a thing it is to dwell in the house of God! But to live content there, it is necessary to understand the vanity and insufficiency of all human things, and to despoil oneself entirely of self-will, the source of every evil; to accustom oneself betimes to treat familiarly with God, in whom alone true joy is found; to be determined seriously to overcome self, and acquire solid virtue, a necessary viaticum for our pilgrimage through life.

He exacted from them the most strict observance of every rule; a total detachment from flesh and blood, and whatever savored of the world; a blind obedience to all that was prescribed; an angelical modesty as the testimony of their interior recollection and union with God; and, in fine, to proceed by the way of love, without any other aim than to please God, and never by the way of servile fear or other human consideration. Neither did he neglect, in due time and place, to prove their virtue by hard trials or public humiliations, and to destroy their self-will by employing them precisely in those things to which they showed the greatest repugnance. In correcting them he was very sparing of his words, but so mingled severity with sweetness that the offender felt himself obliged to amend. And because all are not of the same temper, nor alike in strength of mind, he would call each one separately, and take an account of his conscience, and according to necessity prepare suitable remedies for each one in particular.

By these and other such pious precautions the novices were immensely benefitted, and rapidly advanced in perfection. They looked up to their saintly master as to a most affectionate father, loving him tenderly, placing all their confidence in him, and disclosing all their wounds to him, so that they found their hearts filled with sincere consolation, being excited to new Fervor, and the desire of becoming saints.

How much our loving Lord was pleased with the labors of this His faithful servant, and with his endeavors to train up these young men to perfection, to be in their turn fitting instruments for the promotion of His glory, may be inferred from the circumstance of His so often supernaturally illustrating the Father's mind, enabling him to penetrate the inmost recesses of their hearts, whereby he sometimes delivered them from imminent danger, sometimes comforted them in their afflictions, and sometimes admonished them of the deceits by which the devil was endeavoring to overthrow them. He had one novice of a somewhat scrupulous conscience, who, being seized with a deep melancholy, spent many hours in reasoning with himself and his scruples. The holy master, penetrating into his heart, said to him when next he met him, "Take care, brother, and be advised in time. The devil's aim in exciting this anguish in you is to make the spiritual life odious to you, and so drive you to desperation." He said no more at that time, but kept his eye on the young man, fearing that someday or other mischief might befall him. But a few days later, entering his room unexpectedly, he found the novice in a state of great agitation, throwing his spiritual books, and whatever else came to hand, upon the ground. At this sight he affectionately pressed him to his heart, saying, "Do you not see that all this is the work of the devil? What are you afraid of? God is your good Father, and loves you tenderly. Your fears are all groundless, nor have you any cause for bitterness." The novice was confounded at being thus discovered, but was entirely cured from that very moment.

Another novice was once deeply afflicted about something that had occurred whilst he was still a secular, and his distress reached such a height that he was on the point of forming some bad resolution. Enlightened by God, the holy master saw what was passing in the young man's heart, and calling him aside, said, "Dear brother, why are you thus uneasy? Be assured the affair was so-and-so;" and he recounted all the circumstances of time, place, and persons. The youth was astounded at first, wondering how his superior could have known all this; but guessing that it came from God, he was perfectly satisfied, and quite regained his peace of mind.

Another novice was violently assailed by the devil, so much so, that from time to time his ungovernable fury disturbed the whole house. The superior ordered him not to quit his room, and recommended him with his whole heart to God. One day, as the servant of God was returning home from some visit of charity, he had scarcely put his foot on the threshold, than he was enlightened by God as to the imminent danger of the young man then tempted to self-destruction. He ran in all haste to his room, and found him with a knife in his hand ready to cut his throat. He prevented this, and then, in a tone of great authority he commanded the devil to quit the place, and never to molest the young man again. The fiend was compelled to obey, and the youth was perfectly cured. These instances, and many others, gave rise to a general belief that the superior saw the interior of the hearts of his subjects, which contributed not a little to keep them in proper subjection, and prevented many defects.

With no less care did the servant of God endeavor to instruct the Fathers of the Third Year, —men already mature, and equal to more substantial diet. He gave them spiritual conferences on the most essential points of the institute; on the most suitable manner of exercising the ministry with fruit and propriety; on the necessity of despising all worldly honor and esteem, seeking only the glory of God and the salvation of their neighbor in all they might undertake and accomplish, persuading themselves that going forth to wage war against hell, all the devils would league together against them. Many and great were the dangers to which they would be exposed, so that more than an ordinary virtue would be requisite to preserve them from falling. Their first aim, then, must be to keep up a continual communication with God by prayer, and give themselves to rigorous self-mortification, without which helps they would never do much good.

He inculcated these truths with so much zeal and ardor, that his words were like flames of fire. Whilst on this subject we may relate an incident that happened at Villa-Garcia. Father Egidio Gonzales, visitor of the province, reached the college in very bad health. There was no delicacy of charity which the holy rector did not employ in his behalf, even summoning Doctor Mercati, a very celebrated professor of medicine, from Madrid. He undertook to cure the sick man, and succeeded. In this conjuncture the fathers of the college, who reluctantly beheld their own rector always in a state of suffering, requested the physician to give some directions, and to prescribe some sort of a rule of life for him, to which Mercati willingly agreed. Happening, however, to be present at one of his exhortations, and witnessing the zeal and ardor which inflamed him, he said afterwards to the fathers, "My fathers, this sick man has no need of me; he has a far more powerful doctor than myself to rule him, no other than God Himself."

In order that the fathers who were going through their third year might begin at once to put in practice his salutary and sublime lessons, he did not fail to try them well in various ways; sometimes employing them in the most abject and laborious offices of the house; sometimes sending them to the hospitals and prisons, to instruct and console the unfortunate

PADRE LUIS IN AUTHORITY

creatures there; and sometimes sending them into the villages, to give missions to the poor country-people. Being thus thoroughly instructed, and still further animated by the admirable example of their saintly director, they found themselves, at the year's end, disposed and able to employ themselves with all their power in the service of God and their neighbor, with incredible advantage to the whole province.

With equal ardor did the servant of God, in quality of rector, devote himself to the welfare of all his subjects. Two colleges had the good fortune to be governed by him, —Villa-Garcia and Valladolid, —in both of which his conduct was in every respect worthy of a religious superior. Never did he present himself before God without recommending to Him all and every one of his subordinates and their spiritual profit, that, as he said, it might not be impeded by his own demerits. Moreover, he never undertook anything until he had well considered it in presence of the Blessed Sacrament, and negotiated the affair with God. Most zealous for regular observance, he used every precaution to prevent transgressions of it. On his point he seemed inexorable, having learnt by experience that we easily step from slight to serious transgressions. At Valladolid, having observed that when the sign was given at night, some of the fathers were not sufficiently prompt in observing silence and in retiring to their rooms, he, with much sweetness, but with equal firmness, insisted on an immediate remedy. He would grant no dispensation of the rule without very important reasons, no matter how qualified the individual might be. One of the fathers, going to preach in a neighboring territory, asked, as a favor, to go without a companion, wishing to enjoy the day amongst his own friends. "Oh, no," replied the rector, "Oh, no; why should we omit a rule of such importance in itself, and so useful to us? Go, reverend father, and with the blessing of God recreate yourself and enjoy the company of your friends, —but with a companion." Another father asked his leave to keep a few raisins in his room. "Not in your room," answered he; "it is contrary to our custom, and is not allowed amongst us. Go to the common refectory, where you shall immediately and always have what you require." These things are trifling, as everyone may see, but they clearly show how highly he prized religious perfection.

Besides the rules common to all, he diligently inquired whether each one observed those peculiar to his own office. To the masters, especially of the lower schools, he frequently recommended care in the cultivation of their young pupils, as a thing of the utmost importance to the welfare of the country. When with the students he never spoke but of holy things, and of what might benefit their souls. Besides public exhortations, he saw each one of them in private; and, beginning with the minister, took a minute account of their consciences; so that, all things considered, more than one person used to say that under the government of Father de Ponte people must be saints even in spite of themselves.

At the same time he would suffer no one to be in want of any temporal necessaries. He was the first to moderate them in any excess of corporal austerities and penances, in order that no one might injure his health thereby. If he found anyone suffering from cold, he would take him to his room, and give him some of his own clothes; and when the other, ashamed of so much kindness, seemed unwilling to accept the things, he would say, "Yes, yes, take them, I can perhaps more easily be furnished than you." Insisting, as he did, on the serious application of the young men to their respective duties at the time prescribed, so he was in like manner liberal in granting them every relief and indulgence on the days appointed for recreation.

At all times, whether in sickness or in health, whoever went to him always found him good-humored, and was sure to be received with cheerfulness and courtesy. The hidden faults of his subjects he kept strictly secret, endeavoring to have them amended without observation. In fine, he was most affable with everyone but himself; he excited universal compassion, being in a manner exhausted, scarcely able to stand upon his feet, yet following the common life, and using the common diet of the community, attending to all his functions, whether spiritual or literary, supporting every burthen, without allowing himself the slightest relief.

I will conclude this subject with two or three incidents little less than miraculous. Father Diego Vela, a zealous old laborer in the Lord's vineyard, was indisposed, which made him very uneasy; he was extremely anxious to recover, under the specious pretext of doing penance for his sins. The charitable superior said all he could to quiet him, and induce him to be resigned to the will of God, who knows better than we do what is most to our advantage, but all in vain. "Very well" said the rector, "I am now going to offer the divine sacrifice for you; and know, that the event will neither be more nor less than as God pleases." The Mass being ended, he returned to him, and found him quite an altered person. Perceiving his mistake, he changed his sentiments and language, protesting that he desired no otherwise than as God willed; so much so, that he gratefully thanked the superior, who by his prayers had obtained him this religious indifference and resignation.

In the college of S. Ambrose, at Valladolid, he asked one of the fathers to go and give a sermon in one of the neighboring towns; but the evening before the day appointed this father fell ill. In the emergency it was no easy matter to supply his place. The rector, however, begged another to undertake it, who excused himself on the plea of there being so little time. Father de Ponte, with a smiling face, placed one hand on the father's breast, and said to him, "Go, go and preach; and know that your reverence will succeed better than you think." The other felt himself suddenly changed, obeyed without reply, and on the day appointed preached twice with great applause and success.

As soon as he was appointed rector, he desired that no poor person should ever be refused an alms. During a year of scarcity the procurator went to tell him that they had barely corn enough to supply the house, "If that be the case," replied the holy man, "let the alms be increased." And without further argument he insisted upon this being done. The result was, that notwithstanding the quantity of bread distributed to all the poor who flocked in crowds to the college, not only had they sufficient corn for the whole community, but even a fair supply remaining over and above. This may be ascribed either to the ordinary effect of almsdeeds, or to the prayers and confidence in God of this His faithful servant.

CHAPTER V

He Resigns the Rectorship. Is Appointed Inspector. Serves the Plague-stricken.

HOWEVER unwilling Father General Acquaviva might be to deprive the society of so exemplary, zealous, and prudent a superior as Father de Ponte was universally considered, nevertheless, not to lose him entirely, he felt himself obliged to release him from the burthen of the rectorship. But that the province might not lose the benefit of his counsels, he soon charged him with another office of equal care, and no less profitable to the common good.

The general, in his anxiety for the maintenance of religious discipline, and exact observance of the rules in all the colleges and houses of the order, had chosen from each province three or four of the most exemplary and zealous members, whose duty it was to visit, (simply as inspectors, and without any authority to command,) such a number of colleges as should be assigned them, examining attentively and in detail with what exactitude the rules were observed, with what circumspection and Fervor the ministry was exercised, and finally, with what assiduity and perfection each one fulfilled his own appointed office. If anything required amendment, the inspectors were to consult with the immediate superior and the most influential fathers of the college, upon the most effectual and prompt remedial measures, and in due time were to inform the general himself of all they had observed, either good or evil.

Father de Ponte was one of the members selected for this duty, and to him was assigned the principal colleges of the province. In obedience to the order, he began his visitation in 1598, going first to Salamanca. It would be no easy matter to detail the sufferings he underwent during his journey. A furious pestilence was then devastating Spain, so that every town and territory was jealously guarded, even when free from the infection. The mere sight of the father as he passed along, with his emaciated, unhealthy appearance, at once raised a suspicion that he was attacked by the contagion, so that he was everywhere repulsed, notwithstanding his passports and bills of health. This happened not only in villages where he was unknown, but even in the larger cities, where he was held in the highest esteem; amongst others at Palenza, which city refused to admit him within its walls, and he was obliged to spend the night in the church porch, exposed to the air, and on the bare ground.

He was welcomed to Salamanca as an angel come from heaven. His air of humility and devotion, his manner of speaking on holy things with the ardor of a seraph, immediately enkindled Fervor in every heart. Although affairs were in good order, the superior at once abandoned everything into his hands. With full

SERVES THE PLAGUE-STRICKEN 49

liberty he suggested whatever he pleased for the good of souls and the advancement of religious perfection. He held several conferences with the most influential fathers, who, with his approbation and advice, made several improvements for the more exact observance of regularity, which might serve as rules on future occasions; in fine, nothing more satisfactory could possibly have been desired. During his visitation there was no one in the college who did not consult him and follow his direction in spiritual affairs, and all undertook anew a more perfect manner of life. In the same way, and with the same success, he visited several other colleges, but was detained at Villa-Garcia by circumstances of a very distressing character. Precisely at that time, notwithstanding every precaution, the contagion had reached the town, not even sparing the college. The servant of God was by no means dismayed; being persuaded that God had there opened a wider field for the exercise of his charity, he at once offered himself to assist and serve the infected. Without, then, providing himself with any of the usual preservatives, he went from house to house, consoling the poor afflicted creatures, exhorting them to provide in time for their salvation by settling their accounts with God, offering to hear their confessions and assist them in any manner he could. Nor was his charity confined to the care of their souls only, it was extended also to their corporal necessities, affording them every help, and striving to mitigate the severity of their sufferings when he could not entirely relieve them. He was indeed a subject of wonder and edification to all who saw him.

In the college, where, as we have said, several were

attacked by the contagion, his charity became all heart, all eyes, and all hands in their service. No day passed without his visiting each of the sufferers two or three times, (and the same may be said of the night) spending a long time with them in pious discourses, animating them to abandon themselves entirely into the hands of God their good Father, who would dispose of all for the best, and who would not fail to assist them with His grace, and reward them with an incorruptible crown of glory. It would be easier to imagine than to describe the comfort it was to the sick to be thus assisted and encouraged by their holy superior.

All this, however, did not satisfy him; he offered at the same time to supply the places of the sick. He preached in the church, administered the sacraments, acted as porter, infirmarian, or cook; and when any of the sick died, the humble servant of God prepared their bodies for burial with his own hands. All things considered, it seemed a continued miracle for a man of his delicate constitution, with several habitual infirmities upon him, to have acted, not merely like a man in health, but as if he had been remarkably strong and robust. When exhorted to spare himself a little, he answered, "No, no; since I am good for nothing else, allow me at least to serve others. Would to God that I might die a victim of charity for my beloved brothers; but my sins will not admit of such an honor." However magnanimous his heart might be, his body was too feeble to stand against all this fatigue and little care of himself. The deplorable season, added to the difficulties of his journeys, and his own maladies, which never left him quiet, obliged him to resign his office, to the deep regret of the province, fully convinced of the benefits the colleges had derived from his visits as inspector.

He was not, however, left long to repose. His well-known prudence and talent in the management of affairs induced the higher superiors to choose him for consultor of the province. How well he succeeded in this office, and how useful he was in promoting the general welfare, may be inferred from the good effects which followed. No resolution, no important step, was decided on without his advice; so that, according to the assertion of one of the consultors, during the years Father Louis was among them, none of them ever had to gainsay his opinion.

And with reason we may believe this, seeing that the servant of God was so completely despoiled of every human passion as to have no other object in view than the divine glory and the good of the institute in whatever advice he gave. When any affair was proposed, he implored the light of heaven, weighed the circumstances, and the good or evil consequences that might follow, gave his opinion with all humility, indifference, and docility, being at the same time most ready to change it whenever the contrary, (weighed in the balance of the sanctuary,) seemed preferable to his own.

CHAPTER VI

He is appointed prefect of the spiritual exercises, to the great advantage of the whole province.

NE of the most important offices discharged by the servant of God for several years was that of spiritual prefect in the two colleges of Valladolid and Salamanca; a charge of high interest, and usually only given to men of great virtue and learning, and long experienced in the difficult art of directing consciences. Besides being the ordinary confessor of the house, it is his duty to preside in all spiritual conferences; frequently to give domestic exhortations; to propose and explain at night the subject of the next morning's meditation; to give the spiritual exercises occasionally during the year; and above all to be ever ready to receive, instruct, and console all who wish to consult him on the affairs of their souls, assisting everyone according to his necessities. This office is applicable principally to the larger colleges of study, where the young men in great numbers attend to the acquisition of knowledge, and stand in need of more particular care and culture.

Great was the delight in Valladolid, and in the college of S. Ambrose, as soon as the appointment of

Father Louis to this office became known; everyone immediately placed his conscience in his hands, well knowing how much the holy man was enlightened by God, and how learned, discreet, and affable he was. In truth, the good fruits soon became apparent. He had held the office but few weeks when there was a notable improvement perceived,—a more exact observance of the rule, a more ardent spirit of prayer, longer visits to the Blessed Sacrament, a more composed exterior, the sure indication of interior recollection, a more serious attention to study, the constant exercise, both in public and private, of mortification and penance; in a word, a virtuous ambition in everyone to perfect himself and become a saint. Nor could anything else be expected. His holy words, enforced by his admirable example, were so powerful as to penetrate the inmost recesses of the heart, and were so forcibly impressed, that, according to the general opinion, it was impossible to see and hear him without consenting to do whatever he wished. He was always to be found either on his knees before the Blessed Sacrament, or in the infirmary, serving and consoling the sick, or retired in his room at the foot of his crucifix. Great part of the night was spent in prayer, and those whose rooms were in the neighborhood of his could hear his inflamed sighs, his tender colloquies, and the incessant maceration of his body, oppressed as it was with such continual sufferings. These were lessons which spoke to the eyes of all, and though silent, they spoke aloud, stimulating all to become saints.

Although the servant of God left no means untried to advance everyone in perfection, and to increase in all the desire of serving God faithfully, his chief endeavor, nevertheless, was to devise a thousand means to promote the welfare of the young students under his care. He saw them the most frequently and willingly, never conversing with them but on spiritual subjects, yet doing this with so much sweetness, discretion, and affability, as soon gained him the confidence and love of everyone. That the affection of these youths was not of a mere passing nature is shown by the fact, that when their course of studies was ended, and obedience called them elsewhere, their regret arose from quitting the dear father of their souls, and at being no longer able to receive his salutary counsels and holy instructions. It was quite moving to see them on the day preceding their departure continually running to him to get a last instruction, to implore the assistance of his prayers, and to request permission to unfold their hearts to him from time to time by letter; and then again, to see the holy man, with open heart, make himself all to all, and, like an affectionate father, pressing them to his breast, assuring them that he would ever remember them before God, praying that the good seed sown in their souls might yield fruit a hundredfold.

We may here state that our good God, in order to render his labors more fruitful, renewed the favor He had granted him whilst master of novices, namely, of penetrating with a look into the recesses of the hearts of his penitents. One instance, sufficiently instructive, will suffice. A young student of theology, of very promising talent, tad, under the guidance of the holy man, made great progress in the path of religious perfection; but, as too often happens to persons of his age, his Fervor cooled by degrees, and, keeping at a distance from his director, he was losing all the good he had previously acquired. To conceal this from his holy master, he thought he had better make some show of returning to him, merely, however, to save appearances, and not from any real desire of amendment. No sooner did he present himself before Father de Ponte, than he saw what was brooding in his heart. Fixing his eye upon him, he said to him, "Listen, brother: I speak to those who come to me according to the dispositions which bring them hither. If they come with sincerity, and with a desire to profit by the discourse, I would spare myself in no respect in order to help them; but if they come with deceit, or from mere ceremony, I meet them with coldness, and interest myself but little about them." Hearing this, the young man saw that he was discovered, and blushed with shame; then, bursting into tears, he threw himself on his knees, humbly begged pardon for his fault, and entering into himself, he resumed his former Fervor, and in progress of time became a valuable member of the Society, doing great things for the glory of God and the salvation of his neighbor.

It may be inferred, from what has been already related, how much the whole province was benefitted by the direction of this servant of God, and how much his instructions contributed to maintain in full vigor the spirit peculiar to the institute. As his pupils became dispersed through the various colleges assigned them, they carried with them his maxims and instructions, or, as we may say, his very virtues, copied in their own souls, to the no small advantage of those houses. Moreover, many of his spiritual children made such progress in the path of perfection as to deserve to be remembered in the annals of the Society, as an incitement to, and for the edification of, posterity.

The college of Valladolid was enjoying the benefit of possessing within its walls a man so holy and so dear to God, when he was suddenly removed, to the bitter regret of its inmates. A disturbance arose in Salamanca, which threw the whole college into confusion; superiors sent Father de Ponte thither, as the person most likely to restore order. The obedient religious set off without a moments delay, although he knew by experience that the air of Salamanca was his implacable enemy. On his arrival he was welcomed as an angel sent from heaven.

He found much to console him in the college. The religious were all men of high virtue, aiming with great Fervor at their own sanctification, and the benefit of others likewise; but this satisfactory state of things was embroiled by the vicious conduct of one ambitious, undisciplined, haughty youth, who, not content with straying from the right path himself, endeavored to seduce others, and draw them over to his party, to the indescribable regret of the superiors.

The servant of God left nothing unsaid and undone to bring him back to his duty; the most tender charity was employed, but all in vain; he had too long abused divine mercy to deserve the grace of conversion. Despairing of any cure, the putrid member was severed from the body, in order to preserve the sane parts from infection. Despoiled of the religious habit, the unfortunate young man led a miserable life for some time in the world, and soon met with a death still more unfortunate.

The expulsion of this one restored peace to the college; and the presence of this saintly director produced the same good effects here as at Valladolid,—the same Fervor for perfection, the same zeal for the glory of God and the salvation of their neighbor. In proof of which it will suffice to say, that merely arranging at night, as his office required, the points for the next day's meditation, and explaining them to the students and lay brothers, such was his vehemence and ardor in treating of the eternal truths, and of the divine mysteries, as to cause quite a sensation through the whole house; and all the fathers, even the superior himself, eagerly went to hear him, acknowledging that they derived more spiritual help in hearing him that one quarter of an hour, than from several hours of prayer; and seldom did they leave the place without tears in their eyes and compunction in their hearts.

Before the expiration of a year his constitution gave way under the severity of the climate. His habitual infirmities were aggravated, and his little remnant of health was all but irrecoverably lost; nevertheless, he uttered not one word of remonstrance, nor did he express a wish to quit, being quite content to do the will of God, who so ordained it. It was not so with his superiors, who, when informed of the holy man's declining health and strength, removed him to Valladolid, to the great regret of the fathers of Salamanca, amongst whom he had not spent an entire year. He resumed his office of spiritual prefect, and exercised it during several years, to the sanctification, not only of his own brethren, but of many externs also.

CHAPTER VII

His success in the confessional. His esteem of that function. His skill in the direction of souls.

MONGST all the employments of Father de Ponte's life, none seems to have been more congenial to his ardent charity, or for which he showed himself more anxious, than that of hearing confessions. He had so high an esteem for that ministry, that he usually said he could confer no alms on his neighbor more salutary than it, because it was an immediate work of mercy, and more so than any other, seeing that it reconciles souls to God, and applies to them the Precious Blood of Jesus Christ, with this further advantage, that being a fatiguing duty with no exterior show, it protects the humility of the person who exercises it, and secures him from the danger of vain-glory. With these sentiments well rooted in his mind and heart, as soon as he was ordained priest he devoted himself indefatigably to this holy exercise, giving to it all the time free from other duties, and never allowing his infirmities to withdraw him from it. As from his infirmities it was frequently impossible for him to sit, he would hear confessions on his knees throughout

the entire morning, to the astonishment of everyone. When compelled by illness to remain several days in bed, there was no end to the influx of prelates, princes, gentlemen, and religious men of every order, going to confess to him; nor would he ever refuse anyone, no matter of what condition, thus soothing the acuteness of his sufferings by the fruit derived therefrom. Being unable sometimes to walk to the houses of the sick in order to assist the dying, he would ride on an old broken-down horse, with a companion at his side to prevent his falling off, and was carried up-stairs by the strong arms of others. Our Divine Lord frequently supported the zeal of His faithful servant in a manner quite miraculous. When going to the confessional, or out to visit the sick, it often happened that he could scarcely drag himself along, being seized with such violent spasms as to be unable to breathe. No sooner, however, did he begin to hear confessions, than being suddenly invested with a supernatural strength, he was completely changed into "a new man," so invigorated and fortified as to show no trace of recent pain; and to prove that this sudden change was a special favor granted by Heaven, to second, as we may say, his good-will to help his neighbor, his sufferings and exhaustion returned as soon as his labors in the confessional were at an end. This fact was evidenced by, and sensible to, all who saw him.

Whilst on this subject we may refer to a circumstance that occurred as he was once traveling in Castile. On reaching Valdestella, a town distant about four leagues from Valladolid, he found himself so ill from the effects of his journey, joined to his own complaints, as to be almost at death's door; and on

SUCCESS IN THE CONFESSIONAL

reaching the lodgings was conveyed to bed. No sooner was he there, than a young girl appeared, bathed in tears, who said to him, "Father! Father! come immediately and hear my mother's confession, lest the poor thing should die!'" This was quite enough to make the holy man forget his own illness; he jumped out of bed and hurried off to help her, but notwithstanding all his haste, on arriving at the woman's house, the same child met him, and shrieked out, "Oh, my poor mother! the devil has run away with her!" The servant of God rebuked her, saying, "Child! what is this disgraceful way of speaking? Go on; where is the sick woman?" The child replied: "Ah, my dear Father! my poor mother has died suddenly; the devil has carried her away. Oh, Father! if you only knew what a wicked woman she was! All day long she did nothing but curse and swear, and with oaths in her mouth she has died unexpectedly." At this dreadful recital the holy man was terrified; he humbly adored the tremendous judgments of God, and with the aid of his companion regained the inn, though not without great difficulty. Whenever he related this incident, he always seemed filled with salutary fear; even in his old age he used to say, "It is a good thing for me, that as far as I was concerned the poor creature would not have been without help; if, when called, I had deferred but for one moment, I should have been inconsolable all the rest of my life."

Another favor which God conferred upon His servant was sending him daily some new penitents, to serve as fuel to his zeal for the good of souls. They were so numerous, that without special assistance from on high he could not possibly have satisfied all.

The fame of his great sanctity, together with his ability in guiding souls to perfection, induced many ladies of the first nobility to place themselves under his direction. Although much more willing to serve the poor, he could not refuse others, hoping that by sanctifying each one of them, he should at the same time sanctify a whole family. He made it, however, a condition that, except in cases of sickness, he was to receive them only in the church and in the confessional. The sacred ministry required this of him; and in the holy tribunal they ought only to look upon themselves as guilty. This regulation prevented none from going to him; on the contrary, they were much edified, and willingly remained whole hours amongst the poorest people, being quite content to suffer this inconvenience if they could thus secure the benefit of his direction.

He left his penitents full liberty to consult other confessors, with the exception of some few, to whom he knew this liberty would be detrimental. He never allowed them to make a vow of obedience to himself, being convinced that he thus took from them all occasion of scruple. In the tribunal of penance he was sparing of his words; but few as they were, they were so animating, and so well adapted to each one's necessities, that nothing more could be desired; everyone left him fully satisfied, only desiring to profit by his instructions. His great skill in the direction of consciences, an art so difficult in itself, must be ascribed less to a natural talent than to a celestial, supernatural light, copiously infused by his loving Lord, the better to form him to a ministry, to which a special vocation seemed to destine him for the

SUCCESS IN THE CONFESSIONAL 65

salvation of many souls; a light so lively and so penetrating, as seemed to disclose to him the inmost recesses of the heart, as well as the least movements, inclinations, and affections of those who had recourse to him. It is no wonder, therefore, that he accepted the charge, and with such success, adapting himself and his various remedies to the age, temperament, and state of each one; so that, however great the sinner might be who presented himself at his feet, in a very short time he found himself quite changed into another man. The best proof of his admirable direction was found in the edifying lives of his penitents, who were noticed, and even pointed out, as examples worthy of imitation.

But when he met with certain souls of more pure conscience, and better disposed to receive the impressions of the Holy Ghost, oh! then it was that he employed all his resources, introducing them into the very intimacy of the sanctuary, leading them step by step to the most perfect and sublime contemplation, until, being completely despoiled of all earthly affection, they deserved to be admitted to a more close communication with our Lord, and to enjoy those favors which He usually bestows only on His most chosen souls. To speak worthily on such a subject, I need the heart and tongue of Father de Ponte himself; suffice it to say, however, it was the general opinion that there was not then in Spain a man more competent than himself to discern, in matters of sanctity, a good from an evil spirit, so that he was reputed the oracle of mystical theology; and no one who walked in the arduous paths of contemplation believed himself secure from error and danger until

Father de Ponte had been consulted, and had expressed his approbation.

But as the progress of the scholars indicates the excellence of the master, it will be well to give a slight sketch of a few noble ladies, who, despising the weakness of their sex, advanced, under the guidance of the servant of God, to the highest degree of Christian perfection. The first of these was Donna Louisa di Carvajale Mendozza, a lady of noble blood, of high spirit, fit to undertake great things. She had been Father de Ponte's penitent for several years, and had made wonderful progress. Ardently desiring to signalize her love of God by some heroic act, she conceived the design of passing over to England, and even to London, there to gain souls to God, being fully disposed to sacrifice her blood and life for this purpose. And if unable to do this in a heretical kingdom, in face of a heretical king, it was her intention to persuade ladies of her own rank to enter the bosom of the Catholic Church, and dedicate themselves to the Celestial Spouse by a vow of virginity,—a lily, all the more odoriferous and pleasing to God when it springs up and flourishes amongst thorns, "in the midst of a perverse nation." No sooner did this generous design become known, than it was censured even by prudent persons, and derided as the dream of a distorted brain. Not so, however, thought Father de Ponte, who, examining the affair, not by the rules of human prudence, but in the light of that Omnipotence which often chooses the "weak things of this world to confound the strong," and discussing all the circumstances by the light of prayer, approved it as good, and as proceeding from God. And though for just reasons he did not advise its immediate execution, he failed not to encourage the young lady, assuring her that it was the work of God, who, having inspired it, would remove obstacles, and so ordain matters that in due time she would realize her pious wishes. The successful issue proved that the holy man had not been deceived. In a short time Donna Louisa proceeded to London, and by her zealous endeavors converted many noble young ladies to the Catholic faith, and induced them, as much by her example as by her holy counsels, to consecrate their virginity to God, leading a life more angelical than human, (each one in her own house,) to the scorn and reproach of heresy, and to the glory of the true faith. Donna Louisa lived several years in London, continually gaining new conquests to the Church, and extending the kingdom of Jesus Christ, until, filled with virtue, merits, and good works, she died holily in that city. Her venerated body was afterwards transferred to Spain, and remains incorrupt to this day in the Royal Monastery of the Incarnation.

The second of these ladies was Donna Mencia Padilla, a virgin of noble birth and of most exemplary conduct. She walked, as we may say, more softly, though not with less velocity and profit, in the path of Christian perfection, despoiling herself at once and forever of every worldly thing, and of all human affections. She was a person of exalted prayer, and daily devoted several hours to it, and never lost sight of the divine presence, even amidst the most distracting occupations. To a continual abnegation of herself and her own will was joined such a spirit of mortification that she seemed to be restored to the state of original innocence, everything in her being obedient to reason. One of her waiting women, of a captious, irritating temper, constantly gave her much to suffer, yet she always treated her most tenderly, and never would consent to her dismissal, in order, according to her own remark, that she might always have something to offer to Almighty God, from whom she received so many benefits. Moreover, she treated her body with such severity, that, not content with depriving it of every comfort, she martyred it continually by rigorous fasting, sanguinary flagellations, and rough hair-cloths. Above all her other virtues, charity to the poor was most pre-eminent. All her revenues, and they were considerable, went to succor the indigent. In a year of great scarcity she sold her household furniture, and even her carriage, reducing herself to go unattended and on foot, with no other support than a stick, and this at a time when she could scarcely drag herself along. When left with nothing more to give away, she would have given her very bedclothes, and have gone without herself, if her discreet director had not prevented it. The works she did when seated with her ladies were appropriated either to the decoration of the churches and altars, or to clothe the poor of Jesus Christ. In these pious exercises Donna Mencia persevered to the end of her life. Having attained the goodly age of seventy, she died the death of the righteous, regretted by the whole city, especially the poor, to whom she had ever been a tender mother. Her obsequies were honored by an immense concourse of persons of every rank, all applauding the sanctity of the deceased lady. Many wonderful events are said to

SUCCESS IN THE CONFESSIONAL 69

have happened, in proof of her being dear to God, both before and after her death.

The third, and most celebrated virgin, directed in the spiritual life by Father de Ponte for the space of thirty years, whose virtuous deeds he himself committed to paper up to the time of his death, (for he preceded her to the grave by ten years,) was the far-famed Marina di Escobar, of noble family, born in Valladolid on the 8th of February, 1554, a lady who, for sanctity of life and splendid virtue, was reputed the miracle of her age. It seemed that God would display in her person His power, wisdom, goodness, and, in a word, all His divine attributes. Lest what I say of this illustrious heroine should be ascribed to mere exaggeration, I will only repeat what the servant of God left in writing, in his Preface to the Life of this pious virgin, and for security against all error, I shall quote his own words, faithfully translated from the Spanish: "Our great God and Lord, who in every age, and time, and state, is admirable in His saints, would in these our days elect to Himself a venerable virgin named Donna Marina di Escobar, in whom He disclosed the immense treasures of His infinite wisdom, charity, and mercy, and the inestimable riches of His grace, conversing interiorly with her, and manifesting to her all the mysteries which the Catholic Faith teaches and the holy Church celebrates, in a manner so new, so grand, and so extraordinary, that the favors bestowed on her are not inferior to those which we read of in the lives of Saints Gertrude, Mechtildis, Bridget, Catherine of Sienna, Teresa, and others like them. Since the powerful hand of God is not shortened, nor His wisdom exhausted, nor His charity destroyed. He knows how, and is willing and able to renew the things done by Him in times past, and even greater things in these our times. So great are the grandeurs that our Lord can disclose of Himself and of His divine perfections, and of the things done for men, and so various are the modes whereby He can disclose them, that after having communicated them to whomsoever He pleases. He always retains an infinite number to bestow in so many new ways, as it would be impossible for us to imagine."

To show how well-grounded was his opinion of the eminent sanctity of this servant of God, and with what caution, maturity, and circumspection he proceeded in his rigorous examination of her before he approved her spirit, we may quote another paragraph from the Preface already referred to. He says, "Since it is certain, and fully confirmed by experience, that by the just judgments of God, and especially in these our days, Satan transforms himself into an angel of light, forging and counterfeiting things which appear holy and divine, both in the interior and exterior: nevertheless, I have a moral certainty, as far as I can have in this world, that the spirit that has moved and treated with Donna Marina, and has manifested to her mysterious and secret things, is not an evil, but a good spirit,—not the devil, but the true God, our Lord Jesus Christ Himself,—employing as His instruments His true angels and saints of heaven, and especially the most holy Virgin His Mother. Besides, during more than thirty years she has, by word of mouth and in writing, always given me a most minute account of all that has passed in her, and I, having examined it with great rigor and diligence, have always found it accompanied by all those signs of a good spirit which the sacred writings and the holy fathers require. In the first place, every word, work, and action of the spirit which spoke to her, always bore upon it the superscription of the Divinity, with such wisdom and grandeur, such truth and purity, such gravity and discretion, such sanctity and so supreme a degree of perfection, as sufficed to show that God was the fountain from whence it flowed, because nothing can spring from God either evil or false, light or imperfect, or unworthy of the majesty of so great a Lord.

"Moreover, as the tree is known by its fruits, so did the Divine Spirit manifest Himself in this servant of the Lord, principally by seven rare virtues conferred on her by God, and which are certain signs of the Holy Ghost, who assists those who possess them. The first was a singular purity of soul and body, with a sovereign horror of the slightest fault, and with so rare a gift of chastity as preserved her from every temptation and motion contrary to it. The second virtue, still more admirable, was the imprinting in her soul such lowly sentiments of herself, that in the midst of the many revelations and other wonderful favors so copiously bestowed on her by God, she never had any feeling of vanity or temptation to pride. The third was, the giving her a composure of heart, so constantly attentive to the presence of our Lord, that in prayer and other dealings with Him, she seldom or never suffered even an involuntary distraction, although she spent many hours in this holy exercise. The fourth was an excessive fear of being deceived by the devil in the extraordinary things which passed within her, so that she used all her endeavors to move our Lord to preserve her from all deceit, and not to conduct her by such ways; so much so, that no one could be more eager to receive such visits and favors, than she felt repugnance in receiving them. The fifth was a supreme desire to suffer every sort of contempt and torment for the love of Jesus Christ; and when our loving Lord, in the last third part of her life, was pleased to afflict her with most terrible crosses and sufferings, she was so well satisfied, that she used to say she should much regret to quit this life without having undergone the pain which our good God gave her to suffer. Hence proceeded her most perfect resignation to the Divine Will amidst her terrible trials. The sixth was a very ardent zeal for the salvation of souls,—she would have given a thousand lives to prevent even the loss of one,—and such a compassion for the miseries of the poor, and of all her fellow-creatures, as to feel them quite as sensibly as her own. Lastly, she had a great inclination, though neither impetuous nor inconsiderate, to give an account to her director of all that passed in her soul, never wishing to be guided by her own opinion without the approbation of him whom God had given her to be her master and the visible guide of her soul."

From what we have just related it will be easy to suppose to what a high degree of sanctity this illustrious heroine attained; and at the same time the reader may guess how great a master of the spiritual life, how learned, prudent, discreet, and enlightened by God, Father de Ponte must have been, who, with so much facility and security, could guide the souls committed to his care through paths so sublime as to be scarcely known to most other men.

Donna Marina survived Father de Ponte ten years. How great her affliction was at the loss of so saintly a guide will easily be understood when we say that she herself acknowledged that she owed to him, next to God, whatever there was of good in her soul. Her Divine Spouse did not leave her long unconsoled, permitting her to behold her saintly father surrounded by a brilliant light, and this not once only. He appeared to her on different occasions, consoling her, and encouraging her to persevere in the path she had begun, assuring her that this would give pleasure to God. She died at the age of eighty, on the 9th of June, 1631, a perfect model of every virtue, especially of invincible patience, refined, as it was, by God, with thirty years of uninterrupted and severe sufferings, which confined her almost entirely to her bed. Let us now return to Father de Ponte.

CHAPTER VIII

His talent for preaching and giving the spiritual exercises. His care in performing every action perfectly.

T seems strange that a man like Father de Ponte, of so feeble a constitution, habitually subject to several different infirmities, which left him no respite, should yet have sought out other labor and fatigue besides what has already been referred to, quite sufficient, in fact, to weary even a robust and healthy person; nevertheless, he undertook the laborious task of preaching. The holy man, reflecting upon the immense favors so liberally bestowed on him by God, believed himself obliged to exhaust himself, as we may say, in laboring to sanctify souls, a task most pleasing to our Lord, who sacrificed His Blood for this same object.

Whilst rector of the college at Villa-Garcia,—a small town, it is true, and but thinly peopled, yet resorted to by numbers of youths from all parts for the advantage of study,—he felt the importance of giving a right direction to those young plants, and in addition to the many pious means devised for their benefit, both by himself and by others under him, he would enter the pulpit, undertaking to preach in public, not only during the holy time of Advent and Lent, but also on the Sundays and other festivals of the year. Such was his fame that everyone ran to hear him, and such was the compunction excited in all hearts, that in a few months the face of the country was quite changed. After a few of his sermons everyone seemed anxious to settle their spiritual affairs by means of a general confession. In less than a year many young men renounced the world to put on the religious habit, and not a few repaired to our college, begging as a favor to make the spiritual exercises there, and undertake a new and more perfect manner of life. In truth, it would have been a difficult thing to hear him unmoved, such was the ardor with which he declaimed against vice, and his power of persuasion when attempting to soften the most obdurate hearts. But our Divine Lord was not pleased to afford him strength enough to continue this holy exercise long. Before the expiration of one year he was reduced almost to death's door, and was obliged to yield. Abandoning the pulpit, he could only deliver his discourses seated, and on level ground; this, though less fatiguing to himself, was not less profitable to his hearers. Innumerable were the familiar discourses thus given, not only to the inmates of the college, but also to externs, both at Villa-Garcia and Valladolid.

He was invited to several monasteries, when frequently one single discourse of his sufficed to renew the vigor of declining regularity, and rekindle Fervor which seemed all but extinct. Still richer was the harvest reaped when the holy man gave the spiritual exercises. Everyone knows what a powerful weapon this is when employed against hell, and especially when used by skillful hands. In this respect Father de Ponte was admirable, or to speak more correctly, had received a special talent from heaven. Of the exercises, when given by him, we may say what David formerly said of the sword of King Saul, and the arrows of Jonathan, that "they were never used without taking effect." Numbers of our fathers begged as a favor to be allowed to make the spiritual exercises under this great master. The most distinguished prelates, religious men of every order, nobles of the highest rank, protested that they were indebted to these exercises for whatever good there might be in their souls. An abbot of S. Bernard, to whom Father de Ponte had given the exercises, received such good from them, that he infused a new spirit of Fervor into the whole of his monastery. The Count di Luna, Don Antonio Pimentel, a personage of importance, retired to the college at Valladolid for this pious purpose, and was so enraptured with the discourses of the holy man, that he always assisted at them kneeling on the bare ground, and derived such profit from them that shortly afterwards, being left a widower, he led a most rigid religious life in the midst of the world. But what wonder is it that the words of a man so holy and so gifted by God should make such deep impression in the souls of others, strengthened as they were by that most powerful of all arguments, namely, the example of the speaker? Never did he exact anything of others which they did not see him first practice in the fullest perfection. His own exterior comportment inspired devotion, and clearly showed his interior recollection. It is no exaggeration to say that he always walked in the divine presence, never speaking but with God or of God. His time was so well economized that every moment paid the tribute of some good act.

However common his work might be, he carefully performed it with the greatest possible perfection, so to render it more pleasing to God, and more meritorious to himself. Each action had its own appointed time, found amongst his papers in his own handwriting. This was as a divine law to him, to which he always conscientiously adhered, excepting illness made it impossible, or an express order of obedience, or some motive of fraternal charity, justified a dispensation. He never undertook even the least action without first raising his heart to God, directing it to His glory, and imploring help to accomplish the Divine Will in it. When finished, not satisfied with the two general examens at mid-day and evening, he would, like our holy founder, subject it to a more rigorous scrutiny, examining the motives and the manner in which he had performed it, returning thanks to God for whatever was good in it, as being His gratuitous gift, wholly unmerited on his part.

To do all things with a certain spirit of mortification and penance, his own sufferings, always more or less severe, and which never left him peace or truce, did not suffice; but every action likely to require much time was begun with his arms extended in form of a cross, recalling to mind as often as he could all that his dear Saviour had suffered for him.

He never entered his room without kissing the wounds of his crucified Lord, and the image of Mary His dear Mother. When ill he received no visits of compliments, or if he was sometimes compelled to do so, he shortened them as much as possible by a marked silence, usually saying, "We ought not to waste that time which is given us to gain heaven, and which, when once lost, never returns." When asked to give his opinion on any subject, he raised his eyes and heart to God, silently begging light to give a just answer. The very remnants of time, which escape even holy people, were spent by him in fervent aspirations to our Lord, or in piously saluting his favorite saints. From whence we may easily infer what an accumulation of merits he acquired daily, and with how much truth we may say of him, "Dies pleni inventi sunt in eo."

CHAPTER IX

Some Account of His Writings, and of the Great Good Effected by Them.

WHEN infirmity disabled the servant of God, and prevented his labors for the good of his neighbor, either in the pulpit or professor's chair, he ardently wished to help them at least with his pen, by writing treatises on spiritual or sacred subjects, which might turn to the more universal and permanent advantage of the faithful. Fearful, however, of being deceived by his own self-love, he spent several days in earnest prayer, beseeching God to make known His divine will to him on this point. Our loving Lord did not leave him long unsatisfied.

One day, as the holy man was prostrate before the Divine Majesty, a copious flood of celestial light filled his mind, accompanied at the same time with such a vehemence of divine love, that, overpowered with excess of bliss, and feeling his heart bursting, as it were, in his bosom, he exclaimed aloud: "Enough, enough, Lord! Not so much light, Lord!" He afterwards owned in confidence, when speaking of this affair, that his room at the time became like a furnace.

That this light was also the voice whereby God approved his desire, and encouraged him to put his hand to the work, was shown from the admirable effects produced by this signal favor. These were, first, a sublime intelligence of holy Scripture, especially of matters referring to mystical theology, on which he wrote with as much depth and clearness as if the objects had been actually before his eyes; the second effect, no less admirable, was his facility in writing on such difficult and abstruse subjects, in terms so appropriate, with reflections so correct, and similitudes so just, and all this so clearly and so expressively, that someone more than human seemed to have been his teacher; so much so, that many very learned men asserted that he had rendered these matters more clear and intelligible than any previous writer.

With this assistance from on high, and being assured of the Divine Will, he applied himself to his writing. The first work which issued from his pen was the book of "Meditations" on the principal mysteries of our faith, on the Life and Passion of our Lord, of His Blessed Mother, &c. It was written in Spanish, in two volumes, and printed in the year 1605. It is in truth an immortal work, in which the reader scarcely knows which to admire most, either the extensive learning, or the order of arrangement, or the multiplicity and correctness of the reflections, or the unction with which the mysteries are unfolded. It cannot be read without feeling the will excited to devotion, or without a desire to profit by it. It passed through three editions, and was translated into several other languages within one year after its first appearance. In it he explains admirably the practice of prayer, at the same time furnishing ample materials for it. In it directors and confessors may find wherewith to instruct those committed to their charge. In it religious of every order may find celestial manna for the daily food of their devotion. In it, in fine, every person of every state may learn how to appreciate the eternal truths, and the mysteries of our holy faith, and also how to live well, if they will frequently read and meditate upon them. The pious Emperor Ferdinand II declared that this book had been most useful to him, and was accustomed to say that he knew it almost by heart. Lastly, we may say that most writers who have latterly dealt with this subject have borrowed from Father de Ponte's inexhaustible mine.

His second work, written likewise in Spanish, and published with prints in two volumes in the year 1609, is entitled, "The Spiritual Guide." It treats of prayer, meditation, contemplation, visits from our Lord, and other extraordinary favors, which He sometimes confers on His most chosen souls; of rules for discernment of spirits, of mortifications, and other heroic acts compatible with contemplation, and is much celebrated even to this day. His Holiness Pope Alexander VII, having read it, formed such a high opinion of the author's sanctity, that he would himself examine the process begun for his beatification; and probably, had Almighty God spared the pontiff's life a few years longer, he would have raised him to the honor of our altars. Father Mutius Vitelleschi. General of the Society, a man of great sanctity and learning, never spoke of this book under any title than that of his guide.

The third work produced by this famous writer, entitled "Of Christian Perfection in every State," was written in Spanish, and divided into four volumes. In it he reviews the various ranks which compose the Christian republic, the different states and employments of men, explaining with great clearness, and according to their merits and dignity, their prerogatives and obligations, together with the best manner of fulfilling them.

Fourthly, in 1622 he published, with prints, his "Moral Exposition of the Book of Canticles," in two folio volumes, written in Latin. This work, as well as the Lives of Father Baltazar Alvarez, and Donna Marina di Escobar, (both written in Spanish,) gained the highest praise; and many learned men were of opinion that his wisdom was acquired less by long study, than infused by God for the benefit of His Church. In these works he discusses the most abstruse points of mystical theology, visions, raptures, ecstasies, the true prayer of quiet, and other such things, by means of which God usually communicates Himself to certain souls of special predilection. He explains all these things with so much solidity, clearness, circumspection, and prudence, that these works are of great use to those theologians whose duty it is to examine causes pending for the beatification and canonization of the servants of God.

We have also from his pen "A Spiritual Directory" for the holy sacraments of confession and communion, of the holy Sacrifice of the Mass, of the exercise of prayer and meditation. In this work he sums up in short the most useful instructions upon these matters dispersed through his other writings. Two other large volumes; one of learned advice, in answer to those who from all parts consulted him in their doubts; and the other of letters, full of holy instructions, were left by this indefatigable writer. His works gave universal satisfaction, and were read with avidity wherever they were heard of, and gained such a high reputation for their author, that even in his life-time he was proclaimed a saint, and highly serviceable to the Church. This was the opinion of the venerable Cardinal Robert Bellarmine, who often declared that he found his greatest delight in Father de Ponte's works. In his desire to become personally acquainted with him, he willingly undertook long and difficult journeys. Several religious of the order of the seraphical S. Francis, going from France into Spain, to assist at a general chapter of their order, held in Salamanca, went a long way out of their road to Valladolid, merely to have the satisfaction of seeing him. One of them, the provincial of Leon, no sooner reached the city, than, instead of going to his own convent, he went immediately in search of Father de Ponte, whose very look inspired modesty and devotion. He threw himself on his knees before him to kiss his feet; but the holy man, full of confusion, would not consent, and knelt down too before the other. After a cordial embrace they had a long conference, in which the Franciscan expressed his gratitude and delight at the publication of the Father's works, which he declared had done much good in France. He would also consult him on his own spiritual affairs, asking his direction and advice, protesting that the consolation afforded by the interview had amply repaid him for all the difficulties of the journey. To these courteous expressions the holy man replied with his usual modesty and humility, giving all the praise to God for whatever good the provincial ascribed to his books, all being His free gift, there being nothing on his own side, as he said, but ignorance and sin.

With regard to the utility which his writings proved to the faithful of every class, and at all times, we may, in concluding this chapter, relate what occurred to the aforementioned Donna Marina di Escobar in one of her visions. The lady was rapt in spirit, and seemed to see Father de Ponte in the act of preaching with great zeal to an immense concourse of people. Being much astonished at the sight, she said to our Lord, "O my God! how can this man preach with so much vigor when he has scarcely breath enough to speak?" "Daughter," replied Almighty God, "be not surprised; he preaches to the whole world by his works, and by the admirable wisdom of his writings." And, in the last place, I may be permitted to express an opinion, as tending to enhance the value of the works composed by this servant of God, namely, the circumstance of their having been written whilst he was a martyr to so many and severe sufferings, reduced, as we may say, to a mere skeleton, nothing but skin and bone; in fact, it was the general belief of the physicians that for many years he lived merely by miracle, since it seemed naturally impossible that a man of his constitutional debility could have lived so long amidst such an accumulation of pain and torture. However, we shall revert to this subject in the following chapters.

CHAPTER X

His ardent love of God, and desire to suffer for him.

CHARITY towards God is the queen of virtues, from which all the others derive their value. Hence it was to this that Father de Ponte directed all his desires, all his prayers, all his actions, and all his labors. To render himself daily more capable of this divine love, an affection which only takes root in pure souls, his chief study was, never to displease God, even in the least thing. Although he carried his baptismal innocence unsullied to the grave, he was most careful in avoiding the slightest faults. Since it is a difficult thing to live in the world without being soiled by a little of its dust, he confessed every day with the utmost exactitude, and frequently his confessors could find no sufficient matter for absolution. Twenty years before his death he made a vow, a very arduous one too, never to offend the Divine Majesty by a deliberate venial sin. He observed it faithfully to the end of his life.

His most frequent ejaculation, taken from the mouth of his holy patriarch, was this: "Give me only Thy love and Thy grace, and I shall be rich enough."

He never could find expressions sufficiently strong to testify to God how much he desired to love Him with all his power. He had so high an esteem of the Divine Majesty, that he felt in a manner ashamed to say to God, "Lord! I love Thee above all things!" esteeming this little more than saying to this great, this amiable Lord, "Lord! I love Thee more than a straw!" because, contrasted with God, what are all things but straw and chaff?

Meditating on these words of the Pater Noster, "Thy will be done on earth, as it is in heaven," he said, "I may then beg of God to love Him as the seraphim love Him in heaven." And, addressing those blessed spirits, he exclaimed, his face radiant with light, "O happy seraphim! admit me amongst you, that I may burn with the same love that inflames you; or at least, do one of you descend and enkindle in me this beautiful fire!" At another time he said, "O Lord, my Lord! if for Your glory it be necessary that I should burn eternally in hell, provided this be done without sin on my part, I am ready! do with me whatever You please!" These instances are taken from the manuscript in which he marked down the secrets of his soul. He had the glory of God so much at heart as to have no eye to look to his own. He desired to love rather than to know, and the very knowledge of God, nay, even His gifts, were dear to him only inasmuch as they helped him to love Him better, to give Him greater glory, and show Him more obsequious respect. "No," said he, "there is no honor but the honor of God, and our glory must never be any other than the glory of God." From this great love for God sprung up in him a sovereign contempt for all earthly things, of which he made no more account than of the wind. When he heard himself praised, or saw himself in any way honored, his torture was as great as if he had been amongst thorns, and he looked on these demonstrations of esteem as so much honor stolen from God.

As those who love truly and love much rejoice at being always with the person loved, and to be ever united in will, so we may with truth say of him that he was constantly in the presence of God, almost as if in an ecstasy, and unconscious of what was passing around him. His greatest delight was to be alone with God, giving vent to the inflamed affections of his loving heart in one continued act of love, or else begging the grace to love Him still more and more.

How anxious he was to accomplish the divine will with the greatest perfection possible may be understood from the following passage, extracted from his manuscripts: "It occurred to me one day that whatever our Lord commands us to ask, it is possible for us to obtain; therefore, since He commands me in all things to do His will with the same perfection as the angels do in heaven, I may hope to reach to that perfection, even in the least of my actions, or I ought at least to wish this, animating myself thereto especially by purity of intention, seeking in all things the will of God alone, despoiling myself of all self-interested love, placing my highest honor and delight in desiring nothing but the good pleasure of Almighty God."

His were not sterile desires. Co-operating on his part with the interior sentiments which our Lord in mercy inspired, he thus continues: I rejoice in having an unprepossessing appearance, an unpleasant speech, and other natural defects, because such is the will of God. I rejoice to suffer the temptations I am liable to, and other interior and exterior pains, because God so wills it. If it be His will that I should live a thousand years laden with miseries, labors, trials, darkness, provided I do not offend Him, I will this also. If God is pleased to chastise me with the pains of hell, without any fault of mine, such also is my will. I must equally praise God, and rejoice in His justice, as well as in His mercy, both with regard to myself and others; this need not destroy my compassion for the sufferings of others, because I may deplore what is an evil to them, and at the same time rejoice at the accomplishment of the divine will in its acts of justice."

With these maxims deeply impressed in his mind and heart, he always rested tranquilly in the loving arms of Divine Providence. Whatever happened, either adverse or prosperous, he relied entirely on our Lord, whom he so tenderly loved, saying, "God is my Father, my Mother, my Nurse, my Help, my All. He knows how, can, and will do, what is best for me. If I confide in Him, all will go well. He requires nothing of me that I cannot do. If this or that employment is not good for me, why should I desire it? If He sees that it is good for me, He will take care, and so arrange it; I have only to do my duty quietly."

All occurrences were received by him with equal imperturbability and indifference, in a constant act of conformity to the divine will. His favorite ejaculation was, "May Thy most holy will, Lord, now and forever be accomplished in me, by me, with me, around me, and in all that belongs to me, and in all other creatures." A Benedictine monk, a very worthy man, and a great friend of Father de Ponte's, once visiting him when he was ill, said in a tone of compassion, "How strange it is, how strange, that God, who has health to spare for ill-disposed people who only misemploy it, cannot bestow a little of it on your reverence, who would make such good use of it." The sick man gravely answered, "My dear father, for gracious sake let us leave God to rule the world, as He best knows how." The same religious on another occasion said he had asked some particular favor for him of God. He replied, "What I have most need of is, that the will of God be accomplished in me." Hearing one of his penitents, a lady of great virtue, express the fear she felt of dying amidst the same terrible sufferings which from time to time assailed her in her life-time, being persuaded their intensity would prevent the preparation she could wish to make for her last passage, the venerable man merely answered, "As for me, I ask for no other sort of death than what God pleases. If I fulfil His will I am content."

Whatever he beheld was a new incitement to the love of God; even his own nothingness had this effect, for, finding nothing of his own within himself, and that whatever he had was the gift of God, this reflection filled him with love and gratitude for so great a benefactor.

Whatever fatigue or labor he undertook for the service of his neighbor, he had no other aim in it than to increase the glory of God and extend His kingdom, being ready to sacrifice himself entirely, if by so doing he could make God better known and loved. He could never end a discourse or conversation without some little exhortation to the love of God, exalting its value, exposing its motives, and teaching the manner of reducing them to practice. But, as the most sincere proof of love is to suffer much for the person loved, so he can never be a true follower of Jesus Christ who will not share His cross. And here it was that Father de Ponte's love of God surpassed itself, and clearly demonstrated the truth of those words, "Love is as strong as death." Never did he betake himself to prayer, or present himself before the Blessed Sacrament, without fervently praying for poverty, contempt, and suffering, with this generous protestation: "I desire not to live without wounds whilst I behold Thee wounded." From time to time he took up his crucifix, and casting a look of tenderness upon the wounds, would say, with tearful eyes, "O Lord! give me those wounds! Ah! most holy wounds of my most innocent Jesus, come to me a sinner!" Even in the night he was heard to utter such petitions. It was with this object, too, that he so earnestly entreated to be sent on the mission to Japan, as we have said elsewhere, hoping to be able to give his life for Jesus Christ by some painful martyrdom. Our loving Lord was not backward in granting his pious desires: for the space of thirty-five entire years did He heavily press His divine hand upon him, exposing his virtue to the severest tests.

He was at Villa-Garcia, when on one Good Friday the holy man was seized with the gout in his hands, knees, and feet. The pain was so acute that, being unable to move or stand, he could only support himself by means of two crutches. This most painful infirmity never left him to the end of his life, and from time to time confined him to his bed for several months, when he could neither change his posture or move from side to side. To this was added water on his chest, which frequently impeded respiration, so that he was compelled to gasp for breath. He suffered from such convulsions in the stomach as to be unable to digest his food, which was violently rejected after about two hours of dreadful suffocation; or if a small portion of it remained, it was only for his greater torment, because in the space of a few hours that little portion was changed into an acrid burning substance, similar to aqua-fortis, and caused such pain as made him tremble from head to foot. For several years this martyrdom was repeated night and morning. A burning thirst and a constant taste of bitterness were the effects of these united maladies, to which may be added frequent fainting fits, which from time to time reduced him to death's door. Later the disease formed upon his chest, and ascended even to his mouth, affecting his gums to such a degree that he soon lost all his teeth. It may with truth be said, that with the exception of his head, there was no part of his body without its own peculiar torment, and thus for years did he taste death drop by drop, without, however, ceasing to live.

Nevertheless, worldly people could not enjoy their pleasures with more delight than he did his accumulations of sufferings, for he then felt that his prayer was heard, if not entirely, at least in part. Most happy in the accomplishment of the divine will, he blessed God and His infinite mercy in admitting him to share His cross. He valued this so highly that he would never accept any solace. Among many resolutions found in his own handwriting, one was, never to make known his sufferings to anyone, excepting by obedience. But the most surprising thing of all is, that laden as he was with such heavy crosses, he was never satiated with suffering. To lose no occasion of proving to our Lord how ready he was to undergo any trial, he had drawn up a long catalogue of the afflictions, misfortunes, and miseries to which poor humanity is liable, either from the inclemency of the seasons, the fury of wild beasts, or the malice of mankind; and, after enumerating them all, he thus concludes: "All this, and much more, I ought to suffer with resignation, remitting myself in all things to Divine Providence. And because all this is but little, I ought not to be content merely to prepare for, and receive opportunities of suffering when they present themselves; this would show but a narrow heart. I ought with fortitude and courage to go in search of them, for thus my Divine Redeemer did for me." His conduct corresponded with his words, as the reader may infer from what has been already related, as well as from what remains to be detailed in the following chapters.

CHAPTER XI

His charity towards his neighbor.

FROM what has been said of Father de Ponte's love of God, we may easily guess how much he loved his neighbor; since the two virtues have the same origin, one cannot exist without the other. We may form some idea of the extent to which he carried his charity if we only reflect on the offering of himself so frequently made to God, (as we find in his manuscripts,) of burning eternally in hell for the salvation of one single soul, provided this could be without any sin of his. When any great sinner was conducted to his feet, his heart leapt with joy, and there was no mark of charity which he did not employ in order to gain him to God; he embraced him tenderly, pressed him to his bosom, and encouraged him fearlessly to expose all the wounds of his soul, reminding him that God was his good Father, and that Jesus Christ had died for the salvation of sinners; that if he sincerely detested his past sins, with a resolution not to offend again, he himself would stand bail for him, and obtain his pardon from God; which expression alone usually sufficed to penetrate the hardest hearts, and move them to contrition.

In the application of remedies and preservatives, the holy man perfectly understood what S. Basil calls "artem gratiæ" well knowing that the same remedy must not be applied to all, nor in equal measure. He first duly considered the quality of the malady, the constitution of the invalid, and then prescribed to each one his particular remedy, more or less active, according to necessity, exhorting him to return to him again soon, with the assurance of finding a prompt remedy; and promising, in conclusion, that he would not fail to implore for him from the Father of all mercies the strengthening aid of His graces.

His entreaties to superiors to be sent to convey the light of the Gospel to the heathens of Japan, and the willing exposure of his own life in the service of the plague-stricken, clearly show the nature of his charity towards his neighbor, and his ardent desire for his salvation. Though excluded from the Indian missions, he never betook himself to prayer without warmly and specially recommending to Almighty God the apostolic missionaries in those kingdoms, usually saying that though his sins had deprived him of such an honor, he trusted their labors would tend to the extension of the kingdom of Jesus Christ, and continually acquire for Him new adorers and followers.

In all his employments, as master of novices, instructor, or spiritual prefect, he had nothing so much at heart as to enkindle and increase our zeal for the salvation of souls, often citing the familiar expression of his saintly founder, "Go, enkindle and inflame all hearts." This is the end of our vocation;

this is what Jesus Christ expects from us. He who for this purpose shed every drop of His Precious Blood.

As to his regular penitents, who had entirely placed their consciences in his hands, it would be difficult to describe the assiduity with which he devoted himself to their advancement, sparing no fatigue or effort on his part to secure them the acquisition of virtue and perfection. Not content with having them always present before God, when at prayer he often said, "There is nothing in the world that I would not do to assist the souls under my direction." In proof of which, the so frequently named servant of God, Donna Marina di Escobar, considered it one of the greatest favors she had received from God, to have had Father de Ponte for the director and spiritual master of her soul.

So long as our good God was pleased to grant him health, his life was one continual act of service for the benefit of his neighbor. And as well-ordered charity usually begins at home, his own province, that of Castile, owned itself much indebted to his zeal for a notable improvement in regular observance, in the desire of perfection, and every other religious virtue. With externs he ever made himself all to all, never at any time refusing himself to anyone. On one occasion the porter dismissed a cavalier who had asked for the holy man at an unreasonable hour. When he heard of it, he sent for the porter, and said to him, "May God forgive you, brother. God forgive you. Why did you send away the gentleman? How do you know what his necessities may have been? And if the good of his soul has been in question, what remorse must you and I have for it! In charity, never do such a thing again."

His usual visits were to the prisons, hospitals, and the sick in the towns, always with a view to the good of their soul, exhorting them to be reconciled to God, and to accept their sufferings with Christian resignation. And as fishing for souls generally succeeds better when we give relief to the body, there was nothing that he would not do for them, waiting on them himself, and furnishing them with large alms given to him for this purpose by his pious and more wealthy penitents. His private study, his public sermons, catechisms, instructions, spiritual exercises, and even his familiar conversation, had no other object than to increase the knowledge of God, and to inflame everyone with His holy love.

Never did his charity for others shine forth more brilliantly than when he seemed least able to exercise it. I know of no other saint of whom we read that, not to defraud his neighbor of the help he needed, would be carried in the arms of others, sometimes to the confessional, sometimes into the pulpit, to comfort and encourage all who wished it; yet this he did, not once only, but very frequently, during the thirty years that our dear Lord was pleased to refine his virtue by means of pain and suffering.

A gentleman in a dying state, wishing to settle his accounts with God, and arrange his domestic affairs, under the direction and advice of the holy man, sent in all haste to request his assistance in a matter of great importance. The weather was excessively cold and rainy; Father de Ponte was unusually ill, confined to his bed; but all this could not deter him. As soon as he heard the sick man's wish he got out of bed, not without great difficulty, and would be carried to him.

He spent more than two hours hearing his confession, giving him suitable advice, and so comforted him, that at his departure the gentleman was not only relieved in conscience, and happy about his family affairs, but was also very much improved in health.

Although his maladies occasionally prevented him from either sitting or standing, he could not refuse himself to the numbers who continually asked to confess to him; he would rise from his bed, and kneeling on the bare ground, supporting himself on the edge of the bedstead, heard confessions in this manner for several hours, almost every day, not only without showing either fatigue or weariness, but always with a cheerful countenance, thanking those who thus gave him an opportunity of doing some little thing for the service of God, and the good of their souls.

The many books he composed in his intervals of sickness, and his letters too, were the dictates of his great charity towards his neighbor, whom he wished to aid even after his death. Foreseeing, as he then did, from various indications, the fearful ravages which the dogmas of Quietism, (under the specious names of "pure contemplation, suspension of the faculties, the fixed permanent view of God," &c.) would soon occasion in the Church; principles which, whilst they indulged the soul in a pernicious idleness, allowed the flesh the most frightful license; against all this he furnished the faithful with a saving antidote, whereby to guard themselves from all infection, exposing the guilt and venom of those doctrines; giving at the same time secure rules, drawn from Scripture and the Fathers, how to distinguish the true from the counterfeit gold.

We may imagine how much fatigue and pain the composition of these works must have cost the holy man, especially when we add, that his sufferings had destroyed one eye, and materially injured the other; hence it was extremely painful to him either to read or write. Whilst in this state, he had a little table fastened to his bed; and it really excited pity to see him sometimes looking through several books, in search of the proofs necessary to support the doctrine he was propounding; and sometimes with his face almost close to the paper, writing what he had so painfully sought out, and adding to it his own remarks. When entreated to spare himself a little, in order not to shorten his days, he answered, "Oh, no! this is no great fatigue to me; on the contrary, it is my delight, giving me a hope of being of some little use to my neighbor, even in my old age, and in an ill state of health."

In fine, to sum up all in a few words, I have the ocular testimony of some who lived ten, twenty, and twenty-five years with him, and who all unite in asserting, that whether he were sick or well, they always saw him in one continued act of benefitting his neighbor. How pleasing this was to God was clearly demonstrated by his loving Lord, who sometimes illustrated his mind with such superior light, as enabled him to penetrate the most hidden secrets of hearts, and sometimes so disposed things, that one of his visits to the sick restored them, not only to peace of soul, but even to health of body, of which more elsewhere.

CHAPTER XII

Of his lively faith and constant hope in God.

TO give a just idea of the heroic faith of this servant of God, and show how deeply it was fixed in his mind and heart, we need only remind the reader of what has been already narrated; seeing, that as the Apostle Saint James expressed it, "Ex operibus fides consummata est."

However, to allude more particularly to it here, we may say, that when he spoke of the truths revealed by God, he seemed to see them rather than merely to believe them. They were the constant subjects of his meditations, conferences, sermons, and familiar discourses. Not content with this, he frequently addressed the following words to God, "Lord, strengthen our faith!" In reward of his pious ardor, our good Lord gave him such a wonderful intelligence of holy Scripture, that however difficult and obscure a point might be, he fathomed it, and unraveled the most intricate passages with the utmost facility and clearness, as his printed works prove.

When the discourse fell upon anything relating to the true faith, his face became inflamed, and he protested his willingness to die in defense of any one of its dogmas. That he was sincere in this is shown by his fervent entreaties to be employed in the foreign missions. Whilst he was prefect of studies he never allowed any master to broach an opinion that could at all dim the brilliant light of faith. If he heard anyone propose some new, dangerous, or suspicious principle, he declaimed against it with much power and vigor, giving it no quarter, but exposing all its venom, and the evil consequences it might cause to the prejudice of Catholic belief.

His numerous writings furnish abundant arms wherewith to combat the enemies of the true faith; in fact, no sooner did they appear than they were eagerly read, even by the heretics themselves, many of whom were thus restored to the bosom of the ancient Church, their good mother. From his great and lively faith sprung that invincible courage which led him to undertake, in spite of his delicate constitution, so many laborious offices, and enabled him so cheerfully to welcome his accumulation of maladies, which he bore for thirty years, often saying to himself, and to those who compassionated him, "I know in whom I have believed, and am certain that He is able to keep that which I have committed to Him against that day;" on which words of the Apostle we find this comforting reflection of his own, copied from his manuscript: "It appears to me that God has two deposit chests, well locked and secured, in one of which are deposited the good works and merits of the just, not one of them being omitted, and of this S. Paul makes mention. In the other chest are consigned the evil deeds and sins of the wicked, not one of which passes into oblivion, and of this one God spoke to Moses when, alluding to the sins of his people, he said, 'Are not these things stored up with Me, and sealed up in My treasures?' (Deut. 32:34.) In the last awful day these two chests will be opened, when each one will

CONSTANT HOPE IN GOD

find his deposit in that chest to which he consigned it. It behooves me, therefore, to accumulate a rich store of holy works, and deposit them in the first-mentioned chest, where they are under the charge of Almighty God, who will preserve them till the last day, in which 'He will give to everyone according to his works.'"

His counsels were looked on and accepted by all as so many oracles of wisdom and prudence, which always took their direction and efficacy from faith alone, the light of which he sought as the sure safeguard against all error. Motives of faith consoled him, and sweetened the bitterness of his many afflictions; these motives were all taken either from the holy Scriptures or the eternal truths revealed to us. He usually said on these occasions, "Faith! faith! by this let us regulate our doubts, give strength and vigor to our actions, and derive comfort in all our sufferings."

One of his penitents, a lady of no ordinary virtue, who, however, could not accommodate herself to the sharp capricious temper of her husband, ventured one day to say to him, "Father, if our Lord would only do me the favor to relieve me from the cross imposed on me by my husband, it seems to me that I should very much advance in His holy love." Hearing her speak thus, the holy man, assuming an unusual severity of countenance, said to her, "Lady, do you believe in God?" Astonished at such a question, the lady bowed her head, and answered with great humility, "I do believe in Him, I do believe in Him; it is my glory to be a daughter of the Catholic Church." The father thus continued: "Do you believe that God is Omnipotence, Wisdom, and Goodness itself?" "Yes, I do believe all this." "Believe, then, that God, as Goodness itself, loves you tenderly, and desires your welfare; as Wisdom itself, He has given you this husband, by whose means your virtue is to be refined; and as Omnipotence itself, He will not fail to help you, that your husband may prove no obstacle to your perfection." By these words the lady was effectually consoled and instructed.

From the lively faith of this holy man arose an invincible hope and confidence in God. He treated with his Lord like a son smiled upon by his affectionate father, without any thought of himself, certain that he was in safe hands, and that a special providence watched over him and all his affairs, to which he willingly consigned himself, his life, his health, his honor, his sustenance, his employments, and every concern, corporal or spiritual, great or small, being accustomed to say that he could not doubt that the goodness of God would ordain all things for the good of his soul, conformably with His own promise, "Cast all your solicitude upon Him, because He hath care of you."

His own words will best explain the sublimity of his sentiments on this virtue. He says: "In a particular manner I must most assuredly trust that in all my tribulations, labors, perplexities, anguish, dangers, from wherever they may come, I have only to cry out to God, and He will hear me, and either give me what I ask, or something better; and either give it me immediately, or when He sees it will be most suitable to me. This confidence must be chiefly founded on the infinite mercy and liberality of God, and in the infinite merits of Jesus Christ, because I cannot ask either as a son, or as a friend, or as a faithful servant, but only as a poor slave. Still this poor slave importunes One who is rich in mercy, and who wishes to be entreated, that He may have the pleasure of bestowing His gifts."

His own miseries and imperfections, (which in other people so often check hope and confidence in asking,) only served to strengthen his hope; being persuaded that God could not refuse him what he asked only for the sake of His own glory, and whilst he abandoned himself entirely to His mercy, acknowledging himself to have no merit of his own. "On one occasion," he writes, "I had been much afflicted for several days on account of my sins and passions, when our Lord imparted to me a strong feeling of His infinite mercy, so much greater than all my miseries, weaknesses, imperfections, and repugnances, that these were completely submerged in it. This light left me much encouraged, and emboldened my confidence to ask and expect everything from God, relying solely in this His mercy, and in the merits of His Son."

With still greater energy he thus expresses himself elsewhere: "Being one day discouraged when asking great things of God, because I saw myself so miserable, I was suddenly struck with these words of the royal prophet: 'My soul hath fainted after Thy salvation, and in Thy word I have hoped exceeding much.' (Ps. 118:81.) Reflecting on these words, it occurred to me that I may hope for greater things from God than these, which, (considering my weakness, I could not venture to ask,) so long as my confidence rests on the infinite mercy of God, and the infinite merits of His Son; and thus it is I understand the expression, 'hoped exceeding much.' Hence I may hope for an intimate union and a familiar communication with His Divine Majesty, and other similar gifts, notwithstanding all my own demerits. With this feeling I took great courage to ask for everything without the slightest fear, because if I truly hope in Him, and have recourse to His mercy, all my sins and miseries are but as an atom, which cannot hinder the light of the sun. Neither could I find any cause of vainglory if our Lord should hear my petitions, and even grant me more than I ask, because all springs from His liberality and mercy, and I am unworthy of it all. With this reflection, then, I ventured to say to God, 'Create a clean heart in me, God, a humble heart, a meek heart, an obedient heart, a temperate heart;' seeing that He who creates, creates out of nothing, and has no need of any foregoing merits or dispositions in the subject."

With these heroic sentiments of confidence in the mercy of God and in the merits of Jesus Christ, it is no wonder that he acquired such a composure of soul that no event, either prosperous or adverse, could disturb the peace of his heart, or ruffle the serenity of his brow. Although he deemed himself unworthy of every blessing, yet such was his confidence in God, that he never felt a doubt on the subject of his salvation. In consequence of which, his greatest delight was to speak of the eternal glory of the saints and of paradise. He always spoke of the latter like a pilgrim, who, at a distance from his own country, enjoys calling it to mind, and willingly speaks to others of its grandeur and its beauties.

He endeavored to instill the same confidence into

CONSTANT HOPE IN GOD

all those under his care. When he met with any timid or pusillanimous souls, who were terrified at the sight of their past sins, or who dreaded the difficulties to be encountered in the service of God, or were too sensitive, and unwilling to suffer for Jesus Christ, he would say to them, "What are you afraid of? Is it because your sins are many and great? Is not the divine mercy infinitely greater? Has not Jesus Christ shed all His Blood for you? Has He not promised pardon to whoever asks it with humility of heart? You must confide in Him." "Why, then, are you alarmed at trifles? Have you to fight single-handed against hell? Is not God with you? And if God be with us, who shall stand against us? Come! come! generous soul, advance to the combat!" "Wherefore, too, are you so delicate, so tender? Oh, if you but knew what a precious thing it is to suffer willingly for Jesus! He goes before you carrying His cross; and do not doubt but He will sweeten all the bitterness of your sufferings." By such holy words as these he confessed he was encouraged and animated to run on in the ways of the Lord, and to labor and suffer willingly anything and everything in the cause of His glory.

CHAPTER XIII

Of his profound humility, and other virtues depending upon it.

LTHOUGH it be most true that Jesus Christ invested Himself with our nature, that He might be to us an example of every virtue; it is also true, as St. Austin observes, that He particularly wishes us to imitate Him in the virtue of humility, as being the foundation and basis of all other virtues: "He chiefly proposes His humility for our imitation." Being thus taught this truth, it would not be easy to describe the love Father de Ponte conceived for this virtue, nor the efforts he used to acquire it. A knowledge of ourselves, and of our own nothingness, is essentially necessary to insure success; for six entire months, therefore, did he devote himself to this consideration; and with all the more zeal and ardor, as God, who had great designs over him, did not fail to assist him; illustrating his mind in a particular manner to see that of himself he was but as a mere instrument in the hands of a divine workman. Being utterly vile in his own eyes, it is most instructive to read the indignant expressions he applied to himself,

if perchance the slightest thought of self-esteem arose within him: "Eh! who art thou? what dost thou pretend to? shall the axe raise itself against him who uses it? Quid gloriatur securis contra eum, qui secat in ea?" From this practical knowledge of himself he received, with equal cheerfulness of mind, contempt or respect; and his greatest desire was to be despised, derided, and trampled upon by everyone. And although in the beginning he thought it impossible to attain to this, he had recourse to prayer, when our good Lord soon gave him to understand that all things are possible to grace; and, at the same time gave him hopes of attaining even greater perfection.

In effect, he reached to such a high degree of humility, that though he saw himself enriched by God with such great gifts, both natural and supernatural, as to be proclaimed a saint, and consulted as an oracle by prelates and other most important personages, he never felt the least emotion of pride, or looked on himself as of any value; on the contrary, he faithfully ascribed to God whatever there was of good in him. We find the following words in his oft-cited manuscript: "I acknowledge myself unworthy of all the benefits I have, and of those which I have not; unworthy of the light with which I see, of the air which I breathe, of the water which I drink, of the bread which I eat, of the garments with which I am clad. I am unworthy of every spiritual light, of every celestial consolation; unworthy to receive Him in the most holy Eucharist, unworthy to see Him later face to face. No! I deserve not to live amongst men here on earth; and purgatory, being the prison of noble souls, is not for me; the only place that is my due is at the

HIS PROFOUND HUMILITY

feet of Lucifer in hell." Then he continues, "Supposing, however, that I should fulfil obligations towards God, He would in justice owe me nothing; and should He treat me with severity, I have no reason to complain. Being a slave and a beast of burden, He only treats me as I deserve. In fine, I ought to look upon myself as a sick man, covered with ulcers that infect my every action." His whole life is a proof that his external actions corresponded with his interior sentiments. Never did a word of self-commendation issue from his mouth; so far from boasting of the gifts so liberally bestowed on him by God, he used his utmost endeavors to conceal them from the eyes of others. He never spoke in disparagement of anyone, but, humbling himself before all, he esteemed everyone greater and better than himself. His delight was to converse with the poorest and meanest sort of people; and when he found himself revered and sought after by nobles and other exalted persons, he was filled with confusion, and used to say, "Oh! what a great hypocrite I must be! if they knew me as I really am, they would try to avoid me." His very comportment, his speech, in fine, everything about him breathed humility.

We have already alluded to the eagerness and admiration with which he was welcomed in the schools; no less surprising was the humility with which he exposed and proposed difficulties; more like one who seeks information than one who imparts it. When assailed occasionally in public disputation with sharp biting expressions, he was silent, preferring to seem overcome than to argue for the mere sake of triumph. Possessed as he was of such high intellect and wisdom, insomuch as to have but few equals then in Spain, he would not rely on his own judgment with regard to his writings, either in the choice of subject, or the manner of arranging it, but consulted others inferior to himself in learning, with as much docility as a scholar with his master. The only privilege he derived from being superior and rector, was that of imposing the heaviest and most laborious burthens upon himself. The worst of everything in the house was always for him. He knew not how to command otherwise than by entreaty; and he treated his subjects with so much sweetness and mildness, as evidently proved how completely his exterior humility sprung from the interior feelings of the heart. When obliged, as he sometimes was, to correct anyone, he softened the correction with such expressions of affection that it seemed more like a request than a reproof.

As long as his health permitted, his greatest pleasure was, (as soon as he had discharged the duties of his office,) to go and instruct villagers and rustics in the country, or to visit hospitals and prisons, to console their unfortunate inmates. When already priest and rector he delighted in the lowliest works of the house, sometimes sweeping the church or the chambers of the sick, and of those persons who were most pressed for time, and sometimes assisting the cook, fetching him water, wood, or anything else that he required.

But with regard to himself personally, he was the very reverse of all this. Never would he allow anyone to wait on him, and this not only when in health, but also when he was so ill as to be unable to dress or undress himself without the greatest effort. One night

HIS PROFOUND HUMILITY

the infirmarian found him in such a state of exhaustion that he could not possibly have undressed himself, so he began to help him, when the humble servant of God sorrowfully exclaimed, "Oh, poor me! that this good brother should take so much trouble for me, who deserve not his services."

According to S. Bonaventure, patience is the daughter of humility; and it was so great in him that those who lived with him deemed it almost miraculous. During more than thirty-five years of grievous suffering, never did he utter a complaint either about what he suffered from pain, or from the want of attention in those who attended on him; for this may easily happen in large communities, especially under prolonged infirmity. On these occasions he was the first to pity, excuse, and defend the party. Unless compelled by conscience or obedience, he never spoke of his ailments. He suffered from the piles for twenty years without ever naming it to anyone. He observed the same rigorous silence when threatened with the loss of an eye. The doctor, noticing it, said to him, "Ah! my dear father, what do I see? Your reverence must suffer terribly in one eye, a cataract is forming there." "A cataract, eh!" rejoined the holy man, with a look of surprise; but not another word about it. He showed the same heroic tranquility when he really lost the use of the eye.

Bed, which is usually the greatest comfort to the sick, was to him a torture, even when he was nothing but skin and bone. Notwithstanding this, he lay there immoveable, always in the same posture, and, as it were, on a rack, yet with such a cheerful countenance as to portray no sign of pain. One day, being alone in his room, he suddenly lost all his strength and fell to the ground. Being unable to rise, he remained there for about two hours, when at last a brother went in and replaced him in his chair. When the other, compassionating him, inquired whether he was much hurt, he very composedly answered in these few words, "Blessed be God, who gives me a share of the cross!" During several nights he suffered from suffocation of the chest, because his head lay too low. He said not a word about it, and would have endured it much longer if the infirmarian had not perceived it, and taken care to remedy it immediately.

Once, when much reduced by his accumulated maladies, the doctor ordered that from time to time something should be given him in the night by way of support, on which the sick man said to him, "Remember, sir, I am a religious man, and therefore ought not to occasion all this inconvenience to my brethren." And, in fact, with the exception of the first night, he would not allow it. During his long life of infirmity he would never consent to be under the infirmarian's care, unless his malady confined him to his bed, being content with the scanty assistance of a young student, who helped him a little now and then. From all this we may judge how heroical must have been the patience of the servant of God, who was never better pleased than when deprived of every comfort, and overwhelmed with sufferings.

From his heroic humility, patience, and self-contempt, arose that total detachment from all earthly things which made him believe himself unworthy of every blessing. He shunned every sort of honor and pre-eminence, and was delighted when left in a corner of the house, forgotten and neglected. He used to say that he was much indebted to his maladies, because they saved him from the dangers of superiority. With the exception of some old books necessary for his studies, and belonging to the college, and a few pious pictures on common paper, his room might really be called "the hut of poverty," so utterly was it unfurnished. He never accepted a new garment of any description. He was often entreated to change the habit he wore, as being too old and threadbare, but he only said, with a shrug of the shoulders, "O! why should I turn it away, since it has served me so well for many years?" When reminded that it was time to let an old servant rest, "No, no; I know it serves me willingly." Whatever was given him for his own use, either by his penitents or other pious persons, was bestowed on the poor, and he never spent a single farthing on himself. He would never hear a word about the money arising from the sale of his books, everything being left at the disposal of his superior. Reflecting that poverty was one of the companions of his crucified Lord, who was born and died naked for his sake, it was as dear to him as riches could ever be to a miser.

CHAPTER XIV

His mortification and corporal austerities.

F there was one particular virtue to the attainment of which Father de Ponte directed his utmost endeavors, it was mortification, both interior and exterior, without which he well knew that he could not enjoy familiar communication with God, the great object of all his desires. The better to unveil this truth we will copy his own words. "Perfect abnegation," says he, "consists in a great watchfulness to see and know the least irregular motions of the soul, in repressing them promptly, and in chastising them vigorously in the manner of a valiant soldier, who, when assailed by an enemy, is found ever on his guard, and fights and overthrows so effectually as to deter others from entering the lists against him."

That he might the more easily curb and mortify his inordinate affections, as well as have them continually before his eyes, he reduced them to certain heads, registered in his manuscript in the following terms: "My unruly emotions may be reduced to four; first, in my thoughts and imagination, which are inordinate, either because they are of pernicious or vain things, or out of time, or dwelt on with too much solicitude. The second disorder is in my affections and will, either with regard to prohibited things, springing from pride, anger, envy, or any other vice; or because they are defective in their mode of action, occasioning perturbation, anxiety, immoderate affection to study, employment, preaching, or other such things. The third is a repugnance to acts of virtue, and tepidity in the practice of them, such as are those which relate to the worship of God, to obedience, and to charity towards one's neighbor. The fourth is a license of the senses, in seeing, hearing, speaking; being moved to these things by curiosity, impetuosity, or levity. If in these four points I mortify and deny myself, I shall remove the impediment to union and familiarity with God."

To attach him the more to this necessary virtue, besides other lessons given him by his Divine Master, one was the giving him to understand that his great desire of mortification and vigilance over his soul was an effect of God's love. Nor did our loving Lord omit to teach him in prayer what were the indications of that love peculiar to a soul that is resolved to love Him with all her might. He reduced them to seven, thus found in his own handwriting: "The first indication of our love for God is to destroy His enemies, namely, our sins; to satisfy the divine justice for those we have already committed, chastising self-will, the senses, and the flesh, as authors of so many evils, taking care to offer no new insults to God, using much mortification to effect this. The second indication of this love is to increase it, if it were possible 'ad infinitum,' ever wishing to know and love God better; to remove the difficulties which hinder this, namely, our earthly affections, we must use great mortification. The third indication is, when a soul shows herself grateful to God her great benefactor, the Author of all her good, by being willing to undertake anything for Him, however painful or difficult it may be, even at the expense of her blood and life. Now this point cannot be attained by any other means than those of mortification and continual self-abnegation. The fourth indication of this love is, that the person who loves becomes similar to the person loved. Now the object of this love being Jesus Christ, whose life was all poverty, contempt, and suffering, my resemblance to Him must be effected by acts of mortification, and by renouncing myself in all things. The fifth indication of this love is to do good to and help all those whom He loves; these are our fellow-creatures. Now this can only be done at the cost of much fatigue, suffering, and mortification of self. The sixth indication of this love, (when it is perfect,) is to wish to go, to see, and to be forever united to the Object loved, to enjoy His presence face to face. And because I fear that two impediments may hinder this, namely, not having entirely satisfied the debt of past sins, and not yet having secured the measure of merits requisite to gain the prize, I must seek to remove these two obstacles by calling in the help of mortification, with which I can remove and surmount them. The seventh indication of this love towards God is to conform myself in all things to His most holy will, preferring it to every advantage or interest of my own, and this merely for the sake of pleasing Him. A rich mine of mortification is necessary here. These seven indications, aided by divine grace, which smooths the path, I must continually beseech God to bestow on me."

Our Lord at the same time deigned to disclose to him which were his most dangerous enemies, that by means of the powerful weapons of mortification he might wage continual war against them. He thus leaves them written for our guidance: "I understood, moreover, that this vigilance in mortifying myself, if I really seek to love His Divine Majesty, must be used principally in repressing the emotions of these four passions,—joy, sorrow, hope, and fear,—which are the causes and roots of all the others; and this, not only when they incline to evil things, but also when they would lead me to things which are useless, of no moment, or which do not concern me, or which are mere imaginations, which exist not, and never can exist. All these things occupy my intellect and my will in such a manner as to enervate virtue and spiritual strength, and prevent my affections from being directed to God.

"But when these emotions relate to necessary and natural things, I ought to refer them to God, and never accept them for the mere pleasure or convenience they may afford me; for instance, naturally I enjoy eating, drinking, study, being honored, &c. I must refer this pleasure to God, inasmuch as it comes from Him and is His work; according to the words, 'Thou hast given me, O Lord, a delight in Thy doings.' (Psalm 91.) In the same manner, if I feel moved to wish for health, employment, or other such things, I must take care to desire them as the effect of His divine will and for His glory, in such a manner that God alone may be all my hope, all my pleasure. So also, in moments of grief, or fear of some temporal calamity, I must so comport myself as to fear this danger, or grieve, inasmuch as the cause may spring from my sins, resting solely in the fear of having lost God, or the fear of yet losing Him. Then, proceeding further, there is another means most useful in curbing these inordinate passions, namely, by opposing them with contrary affections; for instance, when I feel a pleasure in eating, in being honored, or other similar thing, I must excite sorrow within myself because I am not treated as my sins deserve, or because they may hinder my progress in the service of God. The same may be said of the movements of other passions. And as it not unfrequently happens that the same thing contains in itself both good and evil, it behooves me to know how to distinguish the one from the other; for instance, that I may abhor honor, as not being due to my vileness and baseness, and yet love this same honor, inasmuch as it facilitates in me the discharge of my ministry." So far the father. These are documents, as the reader will observe, of high perfection, inserted here partly by way of general instruction, and partly for the sake of showing the degree of perfection to which the servant of God aspired.

To this divine theory, acquired by the light of prayer, the holy man joined corresponding practice of whatever was most perfect and most arduous in this exalted virtue. Conscious that he had enemies that would oppose the acquirement of this virtue, it is inconceivable with what vigilance and rigor he fought against them, never allowing them either peace or truce, and this with such profit to his own soul, that in his case the state of original innocence seemed to be restored; every passion following the rule of reason. We may here give the opinion of the Venerable Mother Marianne of S. Joseph, a woman of signal perfection, celebrated throughout Spain, and whose Life, written by the Don Luigi Mugnos, has been given to the press. In her juridical information, given before the ordinary at Madrid, on the virtues of the servant of God, then dead, she thus expressed herself: "It was wonderful to see him live ever at the point of death, yet living to see him so dead to all his passions that he seemed to have none."

I will adduce a single, but striking example. He was naturally ardent and impetuous, yet by offering continual violence to himself he so completely changed his nature as to be thought cold, phlegmatic, and careless. When ill-treated, either by manner or by injurious words, even in public disputation, by those whom his powerful arguments defeated, or by those whose defects he discreetly reproved, he always received the insults with invincible meekness, and bestowed benefits in return for injuries.

Taught by holy Job, he made an agreement with his senses, never to grant them the least comfort or relief, even though in itself lawful; he never would taste any kind of fruit, though it were served round the refectory. Though suffering habitually from burning thirst, it was but very seldom that he allowed himself the slight relief of rinsing his mouth with a little water. He never would go out into the country, to enjoy its freshness, and breathe its purer air. The Count di Luna, Don Antonio Pimentel, wishing to converse with him more freely and at a distance from

MORTIFICATION

all noise and disturbance, begged as a favor that he would accompany him to a pleasant garden belonging to the college, situated on the bank of a river about a mile from Valladolid. The holy man consented; but during the three hours he spent with the Count, he never once raised his eyes to enjoy the verdure of the trees, the brilliant colors of the flowers, the richness of the fruit, or the sweet rippling of the stream. When little recreations were allowed within the college, he approved the custom, and was anxious for all to enjoy it, but denied himself this relaxation, spending the whole time in prayer before the Blessed Sacrament. He seldom left his room or went out of doors, unless from necessity, obedience, or charity. He measured, as we may say, every word, every glance; always on the alert against surprise, and always referring everything to God. During his many years of suffering no complaint escaped his lips; on the contrary, with holy joy he thanked God for admitting him to share the honors of the cross. To escape pity, he strove to conceal his sufferings from others as much as possible.

When the doctors prescribed now one and now another remedy, either to renew his languid powers, or to mitigate the severity of his pains, he would take it under the title of obedience; but if it afforded him a little relief, that was quite enough to make him discontinue it, being unwilling to lose the opportunity and merit of suffering.

Notwithstanding all that has been said, the servant of God was fearful, as the saints always are, lest one day or other his body should turn traitor: he treated it, therefore, with such severity that it was soon in no condition to wage war against him. So long as he had health, he always wore next his skin a sharp hair-cloth which reached from head to foot. He scourged himself every night with such rigor that the blows were heard from his room through the whole length of the corridor. He slept on a bare board, dressed as he was. Besides spending many entire nights in prayer, his usual rest never exceeded three or four hours. His fasting was in a manner continual; he seldom ate anything but herbs; water was his only beverage, and that in such small quantity as scarcely to amount to three ounces. At length, his superiors, out of compassion for his health, were obliged to put him under obedience to one of his subjects with regard to his penances, (and this even when he was rector,) in order to moderate the excessive rigors which were undermining his constitution and materially shortening his days. It is true his austerities were moderated, but his health was destroyed; whilst his desire of mortification increased daily, it certainly was wonderful to see him reduced to a mere shadow, with scarcely a remnant of life, with strength, as we may say, to do nothing, except to torture himself; resting on the edge of his bed he disciplined himself so unmercifully that the floor of his room was sprinkled with blood. But who will believe that all this mortification did not satisfy him? It may seem incredible, nevertheless he went so far as to rejoice at finding in God, not mercy alone to pardon his sins, but just vengeance to punish them: "I am consoled, O Lord," these are his words, "that Thou shouldst be glorified by exercising Thy justice upon me. Chastise my haughtiness, my vanity, my ambition, my hypocrisy, that Thy honor, which I have outraged, may be fully repaired."

After such expressions as these, any comment of ours would indeed be feeble.

CHAPTER XV

His great purity of soul and body.

 FTER this account of the manner in which Father de Ponte treated his body, and the austerities with which he afflicted it to the end of his life, the reader might with reason suppose that he had not always been innocent and faithful to God, and that with him, as with many of the saints, it was necessary to efface past sins by present penances.

He carefully endeavored to avoid even the slightest faults; but when, through human frailty, he did commit some small defect, he hastened to repair it by sacramental confession, in order that sin might be a stranger to him, without a chance of ever becoming the inmate of his soul. Several witnesses who lived with him ten, twenty, and twenty-five years, declared on oath that though they attentively observed him, they never knew him guilty of a fault or even an imperfection: on the contrary, in every action he always seemed to choose that which was most perfect.

He was so vigilant in guarding against even the shadow of a fault, that he suspected defect where defect was not, and tortured, as we may say, every movement of his heart. His own words will best explain this. "I find there are four evil intentions which combat against my spiritual duties. The first is vanity, desiring that others should look upon me as a spiritual person. The second is curiosity, wishing to experience in myself a sensible feeling of God, celestial illustrations, raptures, ecstasies, more for the sake of a practical knowledge of these things than for the glory of God. The third is spiritual sensuality, desiring relish, consolations, tears, &c. The fourth is self-interest, wishing for light, progress, and spiritual favors with eagerness and perturbation, more to be freed from the torment of spiritual poverty than to honor God." He then concludes with this heroic resolution: "I must therefore animate myself to do all things with purity of intention, as an angel would do them, seeking only the will of God for His own sake, despoiling myself of all self-love, of all self-interest, whether spiritual or temporal.'" This being presupposed, it is no wonder that, confessing as he did every day, his confessors should have found it difficult to find matter for absolution.

But in my opinion nothing gives a better idea of his purity of conscience than the celebrated vow he made twenty years before his death, of never committing any deliberate venial sin. Whoever reflects on all the circumstances of human frailty, ever inclined to evil, and of the hundred and thousand occasions of transgressing which meet one at every step, will realize the difficulty of always standing firm without ever slipping. If, too, even the just meet with we know not how many falls, who is there that keeps so strict a guard over himself that he does not

PURITY OF SOUL AND BODY

sometimes utter an idle word, or give one incautious glance? Who is there that so well economizes time as never to lose a single moment? Who, in fine, holds such despotic dominion over all his passions and affections, as to promise himself never to transgress the limits of duty, in thought, word, or deed? Notwithstanding all this, the holy man observed this arduous vow perfectly for twenty years, insomuch that his confessors could never detect in him the slightest deviation from it.

With regard to his chastity and purity of body, it may with truth be affirmed, (according to the declaration of his directors,) that from his earliest years, and through the whole course of his life, he lived more like an angel than a man. In proof of this we may remark that after his death, on looking over the manuscript in which he was accustomed to note down his defects, there was not found in it one single allusion to this subject, not a fugitive glance of the eye, not a passing thought, not an incautious word. He lived and died a virgin. Nor is this surprising, for, besides having in childhood placed his virginity in the hands of our Blessed Lady, and continually recommended it to God, well knowing that chastity is so delicate a virtue that a mere trifle often dims its luster, he guarded it with such jealousy, circumspection, and industry, that it was as secure as a pearl in its shell, or a lily surrounded by thorns. Never would he consent to see any ladies out of the confessional, even in the church, nor did he ever look in the face of any of them, not even his sister or his mother. When visiting sick ladies he insisted on his companion being in sight. He admitted no useless compliments, but began at once to converse on the affairs of their conscience, and having instructed and consoled them, heard their confession, and given them absolution, he withdrew.

Everyone knows how difficult it is under long infirmity, where the invalid suffers from several complaints, weakened to the last degree, and in constant need of assistance, how difficult it is, I say, to keep strict custody over the body, so that no part of it be exposed to the eye of another. Nevertheless, Father de Ponte, during his thirty years illness, was so guarded and circumspect, that neither the infirmarian nor any others who assisted him ever saw him otherwise than modestly covered in every respect. Being unable to dress or undress himself without great pain and difficulty, he had his under garments so contrived as to slip on and off without the assistance of a second person, so great was his modesty. It may scarcely seem credible, but so particular was he in this respect, that he never saw his own feet uncovered, even to pare his nails, which occasioned him a martyrdom, since they grew to such a length as to turn back under his toes, like the claws of a bird; but he would not yield, lacerated as his feet were. This was never known till after his death, when his body was prepared for burial. Lastly, the rigorous austerities he inflicted on himself, both in sickness and in health, were chiefly intended to prevent his body from being an obstacle to this virtue, so dear to him, in defense of which there was no martyrdom that he would not willingly have undergone.

CHAPTER XVI

His prayer and sublime contemplation.

THAT Father de Ponte's prayer may with truth be said to have been continual, is attested by his internal and continuous union with God, even amidst the most distracting occupations. Nevertheless, he took care to assign it a due portion of time, usually during the night, when the soul, undisturbed by exterior objects, is better disposed to receive heavenly impressions. When others retired to rest, he repaired to the church, where, on his knees, or if debility prevented him from kneeling, seated on a low wooden stool, without any kind of support, and with his head uncovered, his hands either joined or crossed upon his breast, he began his prayer before the Blessed Sacrament, continuing it for several hours, often until the end of the morning meditation, common to all the rest. When severe infirmity rendered him unable to go to the church, he prayed in the same manner in his room, with this only difference, that when he was in the church he prayed in silence to escape observation, repressing within himself the affections which carried him so violently to God. When shut up in his own room, free from all subjection, he gave full vent to his inflamed heart in sighs, tears, exclamations, and sweet colloquies with his Divine Lord.

He followed the method of prayer prescribed by S. Ignatius in his golden book, the Spiritual Exercises, in which the soul employs its three powers on divine things, until the intellect being convinced by reasoning of the truths presented by the memory, the will is disposed to produce affections suitable to the subject, and resolutions necessary for the amendment of life, which is the sole object to be aimed at. Admirable was the humble attitude, as well as the profound reverence, with which he presented himself before the Divine and Tremendous Majesty, on his knees with his face bowed to the earth, inviting all creatures to adore and praise so great a Lord, using the words of holy David, "Venite adoremus et procedamus ante Deum."

Almighty God, who can easily "make the poor man suddenly rich," delighting in a soul so pure and humble, showed Himself no despotic Master; but no sooner beheld him at His feet, than He speedily drew him to Himself, admitting him to a share of His divine treasures; communicating Himself to him by all those ineffable ways which He uses with His most chosen souls. Hence, the holy man being admitted to this familiar communication with his Lord, and consoled by clear and copious light to contemplate so closely the amiabilities of this Infinite Good, the admirable means of His inscrutable providence, the economy of human redemption, and His other wondrous attributes, became all love for Him, and overpowered by such an abundance of sweetness, he fell into

PRAYER AND CONTEMPLATION 133

transports of tender devotion. One instance will suffice to explain this. The servant of God being at prayer in his room, suddenly felt his mind filled with a light so penetrating and lively, that his heart was inflamed to such a degree, that, unable to restrain the celestial ardor, he hastily rose from the ground and ran about his room, crying out aloud, "Not so much light! not so much light! It is enough, O Lord! it is enough! no more!"

Such incidents were not of rare occurrence. Whenever he betook himself to prayer, sensation seemed lost; he was absorbed in such sweet ecstasies, that his body, influenced by his soul, was raised several palms from the ground. At the end of his prayer he was often seen descending to the garden, where he gave free vent to the feelings of his heart, in affectionate aspirations and tender colloquies with his Lord. He seemed little less than a seraph. He sometimes remained during a whole day so immersed in the contemplation of the Divine Greatness, that nothing in the world could distract him. Once when he was walking out, a furious bull ran at him, and in its rage was going to attack him. People cried out aloud to warn him of the danger, but he heard nothing, saw nothing; fortunately his companion dragged him away by main force, or he would certainly have been seriously wounded, and perhaps killed. Being asked if he was not terrified, he unconsciously said, "Of what? of what?" He had no idea of what had occurred to him.

The reader must not expect me to describe in detail the sublime intelligence of divine things conferred on the holy man in his high contemplations, or the ineffable sweetness he imbibed at the fountain head of the Divinity, or the frequent visions and other favors which our Lord was pleased to bestow with such liberality upon His servant. This would be to lose myself in a mist, or fall into a boundless sea. Suffice it to say, that whatever appears in his writings, as passing between the soul that loves God, and God Himself, he had first experienced it; therefore it was with reason that he gained the reputation of being one of the first masters of mystical theology, and one of the most sublime contemplatives then in the Church.

I may, however, be allowed to give some of his own reflections found amongst his papers; they will enable us to form an idea of his virtue, and at the same time instruct us how, and with what goodness, our Divine Lord treats those souls who faithfully serve Him. After amply describing the happiness of a soul that sees itself united to the Divine Omnipotence, surrounded on all sides by it, with the sweet effects it produces, one of which is, to infuse into it a generosity and greatness, to undertake great and heroic things in the service of God, and to suffer any trial, no matter how great, for love of Him; he passes on to say, that to acquire this union, which he calls unspeakable, the straight path is no other than that of self-abnegation; and it is in this sense he understands and explains these words of holy David, "Eo quod non cognovi literaturam introibo in potentias Domini;" as if he had said, "Because I did not seek to appear wise, nor glory in the human knowledge I possess, I shall enter into the power of the Lord; I will confide in His Omnipotence, and shall be strong in it;" then he adds, "Unless the learned of this world become ignorant by choice, never will they enter into the power of the Lord." In effect, this was the way by which this servant of God reached so high a degree of contemplation, and acquired that ineffable union whereby our Lord united him to Himself. He continually wished to be looked upon by everyone as a vile incapable creature, fit for nothing; and always bore in mind the saying of our Divine Redeemer to the holy virgin, S. Catherine of Sienna, "I am what I am; thou art what thou art not." From which he inferred, that since he was what he was not, that is, nothingness, it was highly important to keep himself united to Him who is, and who is all in all; as from this union every good comes to us. In recompense for this disposition, God was pleased to give him clearly to understand the strict union He had with him, with regard to his undertakings, to which he himself refers in these precise terms: "It appears to me that God dwells within me, so united in action, that being two, we seem but one; whilst I never undertake anything, but He also acts with me."

On another occasion, when he was contemplating the strength of the divine Omnipotence, which when united to man raises him above himself, and in a certain manner deifies him, there arose in his heart such a strength and vigor, with such confidence of being able to do great things for the glory of God, that he gave utterance to these expressions, "If God is omnipotent, and out of love unites Himself with His omnipotence to man, this man also becomes omnipotent by participation of His power. His prayer is omnipotent, to obtain whatever he asks of God; his obedience is omnipotent, to execute whatever God commands; his patience is omnipotent, to suffer whatever trials God sends; so also is his charity, his zeal, his fortitude, and every other virtue, so that he may say with the Apostle, 'I can do all things in Him who strengthens me.'" With this reflection he encouraged his magnanimous heart to undertake, whether sick or well, such great labors for the sake of his neighbor, and to suffer cheerfully such grievous pains, ever aspiring to the acquisition of the greatest possible perfection.

Another fruit of his contemplation was the following instruction, which we give in his own words: "I find three methods of the presence of God; the first is, His presence in the Blessed Sacrament, and this can serve us only in the Church; the second is, to consider Him as present throughout the whole world, and in the place where I am, and myself in Him, as a fish in the water; to consider Him in this manner offers no impediment to the eyes being held open; light is no inconvenience, nor the sight of creatures either, because all is seen in God. 'In Him we live, move, and are.' The third manner is to behold God within myself, because He really dwells in me, 'Thou art in the midst of us, O Lord.' And then insensibly the eyes close, and becoming wholly recollected within oneself, all our powers are directed to God alone, speaking to Him, and seeking to be united with Him. This method is well suited to union with God, and to draw affections of joy and confidence, beholding the greatness which the soul contains within itself. This divine presence is attained by three kinds of acts. The first, acts of faith, meditations, discourses, and a simple comprehension of the divine presence being in every place, and in our own hearts. The second, petitions; because whoever asks of another asks of one who is actually present, no one speaks to an absent person. The third by affections, acts of love, joy, praise, &c., and this is the most sublime manner, because no one thing can be more present to another than when the two are united and attached together."

With what perfection he himself practiced what he has left us in writing, was well known to those who lived with him, who assert his mode of life to have been such as clearly showed that he never lost sight of his loving Saviour. Often during the day he was seen to raise his eyes and hands to heaven, as if delighting in God. At other times he gave demonstrations of surprise, as if experiencing some unusual favor; then again, he would break out in tender ejaculations, indications of the love which burned in his heart. Sometimes he recited passages from holy Scripture, expressive of the infinite power and wisdom of God; thus giving us to understand that He was the sole object of his love. Above all, whatever he saw or heard, he drew a moral for his neighbor's profit.

Giving an account elsewhere of the things he continually begged of God in his prayers and contemplations, he reduces them chiefly to these four: 1. A great light, whereby to know God, himself, and those who were under his care and direction; 2. An ardent disinterested love of God, caring for nothing else in the world; 3. A great hatred of himself, with a great love for crosses, contempt, and sufferings; 4. An ardent zeal for the divine glory and the salvation of souls. That he might the more easily obtain what he asked, he recommended the first to our Blessed Lady, the second to S. Joseph, the third to S. John Baptist, and the fourth to the Apostle S. Paul, honoring each one of them daily, practicing some devotions in their honor, the more surely to gain their favor. Then, turning to his angel guardian, he said, "O my good angel! I confide all to thee; in thee I hope; beseech these my dear advocates to intercede for me; and do thou treat of my affairs immediately with God."

These, however, were not the only favors the holy man implored of God in prayer, well knowing that He is rich in mercies, and most liberal in bestowing them. I find eight others registered in his manuscript of memorandums: he begs light to know, 1st, God and His greatness, especially His presence in every place; 2ndly, Jesus Christ, and His riches, and in particular His presence in the Blessed Sacrament; 3rdly, His own wicked self, and his own miseries; 4thly, The world, and the vanity of its honors, riches, and all its other goods; 5thly, Souls, and how great their value; 6thly, The blessings we have received from God, and those which we hope to receive from Him; 7thly, The evils and chastisements that we have reason to fear; 8thly, and finally, To know the divine will in all things.

To conclude this chapter then, we may say, that frequent were the visions with which God honored him for his own and others' good, teaching him most important truths by mysterious symbols; as the manner of acting under distractions, labors, temptations, and other similar things, belonging more particularly to ascetic writings, and therefore unnecessary to the historian.

CHAPTER XVII

His obedience and zeal in the observance of his institute.

HAVING shown with what perfection Father de Ponte observed the divine precepts, the evangelical counsels, and whatever else the Church prescribes, it can easily be imagined how exact was his obedience to the laws of the institute which he professed. Convinced that this virtue is the soul of religious life, he signalized himself in it like a true follower of Jesus Christ, who lived and died by obedience; showing himself ready on many occasions to lose his life rather than deviate from it in the least point.

At Villa-Garcia, when he was appointed to the important offices of master of novices, rector, and instructor of those young fathers going through their third year of probation, his delicate constitution soon felt the effects of these multiplied engagements, and threatened to sink beneath the burden. Exhorted to apply to superiors for at least some partial relief, he replied, "No indeed! never could I do such a thing! obedience has placed me here, and here will I remain, even if it cost me my life. Superiors hold the place of

God, and know better than I do what suits me. Let death come: I can desire no better death than that of obedience, seeing that Jesus Christ has given me the example of it. 'He was made obedient unto death, even the death of the cross.'"

These sentiments encouraged him to remain firm at Salamanca on two several occasions, although he knew by experience how injurious the climate was to his health. He said: "That I should live is not necessary, but it is very necessary that I should obey, if I wish to be a good religious." "The Lord governs me." Relying on these words he waited till his superiors, of their own accord, ordered him elsewhere for the sake of his health.

Everyone knows how numerous and minute religious rules are, nevertheless, those who lived with him for many years declared on oath that they had never observed him willingly transgress anyone of them. So long as he could drag himself along on two crutches, he would never accept dispensations from any functions of the community. After spending many hours in prayer before the others arose in the morning, he always made the common meditation with them at the hour assigned by obedience. That he might not lose the merit of this virtue, even in the least things, he would go and ask the most trifling permissions of superiors: when the companion who had charge of his health advised him to spare himself this inconvenience on account of the general permission he had, he answered him, "Oh, brother! let me perform these acts of submission to my superior, who holds the place of God. With this subjection I may hope to become more pleasing to His divine

Majesty, and render my actions more meritorious to myself."

He practiced this subordination and dependance, not only towards superiors, but even to the lowest subordinate official in the house. When humility led him to assist the infirmarian, or the cook, or any other, he obeyed them with the utmost punctuality and exactness in whatever concerned their offices. And because higher superiors, for the sake of his health, had subjected him to one of the brothers, he looked upon him as his master, and followed his orders with such humility and promptitude that the brother was confounded and edified.

Whenever it happened that his superiors thought differently from him, he immediately renounced his own opinion; never would he suffer anyone to censure them in his presence. Whilst he was superior, condescending as he was in granting permissions, he was far from being pleased when he saw any of his subjects seeking to follow their own fancies and caprices, which, if not promptly checked, will most certainly lead to the destruction of all regular observance.

In the many heavy trials which the Society underwent in his time, he never lost his peace of heart or serenity of countenance. He used to say, "These are all dispensations of God, which we must obey and submit to. Nothing of this happens but by His will." In these cases, however, his humility led him to think that the afflictions of the order were the chastisements of his own sins; hence he prolonged his prayers, increased his fasts, redoubled his penances, in order to appease Divine Justice, irritated, as he said, by his sins.

With regard to the institute, such was his esteem of it, that he considered it little less than a divine law, written by the finger of God, and consigned by Him to our saintly lawgiver; frequently recalling to his mind the celebrated saying of Pope Paul III when he approved it, "The finger of God is here." He left no means untried to maintain it in its full vigor. To this effect he let slip no occasion of recommending the study and observance of it; demonstrating from time to time in his domestic exhortations, conferences, and in the spiritual exercises, the symmetry of the whole edifice, the proportions of its various parts, and other admirable properties peculiar to it; all which contributed much to raise our esteem of it.

Whenever he saw any serious failing against the rules, seized with a holy zeal, he either applied a remedy himself, or if this did not suffice, he informed higher superiors of it by letter, that their authority might provide an antidote; at the same time suggesting to them with great judgment, charity, and discretion, the method best calculated to insure success. From thence arose that high esteem of his zeal, prudence, and learning, which all the generals who ruled the Society in his time had of him; they frequently applied to him by letter, asking his advice with regard to the most intricate and difficult affairs of the whole order, and remitting the execution of the decisions to him in several of the provinces.

CHAPTER XVIII

Of his devotion to the Blessed Eucharist.

UNDERTAKING, as I am, to describe the tender devotion of the servant of God to the most Holy Sacrament, I must own I find myself unable to express how great it was. I may with truth affirm that this was his strongest predominant passion. Convinced by faith that in the consecrated Host there really exists the same Divine Lord who was incarnate of the Virgin Mary, and who constitutes the beatitude of the angels and saints in heaven, he never presented himself before Him but with his face bent to the ground. The reflection that Jesus Christ instituted this divine sacrament from an ardent desire to be with us, giving Himself to us as food, that He might in a manner deify our flesh, and make us one with Him, made his whole heart overflow with love. "Is it possible," said he, "O my good Jesus, that a God of so great majesty as Thou art should so love us, Thy vile creatures, as to be unwilling to be without us? Since heaven consists in living with Thee and by Thee, what can I desire more than I have here? This is my paradise; 'it is good for us to be here.'"

Deeply impressed with this truth, he seemed unable to live without his sacramental Lord, so frequent were the visits whereby he would adore Him. Every remnant of time left free from the duties of his charge was sure to be spent before the altar of the Blessed Sacrament. Whenever anyone wanted him, and did not find him in his room, he had only to seek him in the church, secure of finding him in prayer before the Holy of Holies. On these occasions, so profound was his consideration of this divine mystery, that calling him was not sufficient to arouse him, it was frequently necessary to push or shake him.

Great as was the esteem and love which this holy man had ever felt towards this sweet sacrament, it was increased beyond measure by meditating one day on this verse of the 117th Psalm: "Open ye to me the gates of justice: I will go into them, and will give praise to the Lord." He thus expresses himself on this subject: "In these gates of justice were represented to me the principal devotions by which we acquire perfection, and I understood the first of these to be Jesus Christ in the Blessed Sacrament, who says of Himself, 'I am the door; if anyone enters by Me he shall be saved, and shall go in and out, and shall find pasture.' And O! what a door this is! At my first entrance I meet with three admirable examples of virtue, which our Lord gives me in this most wonderful Sacrament, examples which, being present and not past, have more power to move me. The first, of consummate humility, covering His own infinite greatness under so vile a form as that of bread, which is the reason why so many do not know Him, whilst others despise and trample on Him, and others again treat Him with so little reverence. O my God and my King! by how much the more vile Thou art for me, so much the more dear Thou art to me! The more Thou dost humble Thyself, the more will I love, praise, and exalt Thee. The second example is of obedience, descending from heaven at the voice of the priest the moment he finishes the word of consecration, even if the priest be an impious, sacrilegious man. And Thou, my good Jesus, art thus cast on the dunghill, and remainest there until the sacramental species are consumed. Thou hast said, too, 'I came down from heaven, not to do My own will, but His who sent Me. This also is the will of My Father, that he who comes to Me should not be cast forth.' The third example is of mercy, abasing Himself with man to exercise all the works of mercy." Here the holy man explains at length how this happens, which for the sake of brevity we omit. He adds in continuation, "If, on entering this door, I gird myself with these three virtues, and with an ardent desire of imitating Jesus in them, He will allow me to advance further, to where the plenitude of His justice dwells, which is His infinite charity; 'love is the plenitude of the law.'" To these considerations he adds another of no less weight, the better to inflame his love towards this August mystery.

"One day," says he, "after Mass, beseeching our Blessed Lady, as my guide, to infuse into my heart some feeling similar to those which she experienced in her communions, I was given to understand that every time she communicated, the same relish, sentiments, and gifts were renewed as had been given to her when she conceived her Son by the operation of the Holy

Ghost. And I understood that although Christ our Lord dwelt in the bosom of Mary alone, by choosing her for His Mother, for which reason He had imparted to her so many and such exalted gifts, yet His Divine Majesty would nevertheless in this sacrament really enter into the breasts of all the faithful, desirous that all should receive Him in the same manner, and proportionately with the same dispositions and the same welcome as His Divine Mother received Him, since He was disposed to confer similar graces on them to those conferred on her; for the entrance of Jesus Christ into the breast of the communicant is but an imitation of His entrance into her pure womb, and He wishes everyone to participate in His gifts."

Overpowered by the vastness of such a gift, and anxious to testify his gratitude to his Divine Benefactor, he thus continues: "I must, then, in the first place excite in myself a great hunger for this celestial food, and an ardent desire to receive it, with a preparation suited to so great a guest, and afterwards thank Him most fervently for so signal a benefit. In the second place, I must wish and endeavor to remain in His company as much as I can, both by day and night; I must visit Him often, adoring Him in every church I pass. And finally, I must have a great respect for everything connected with this most holy mystery."

These generous purposes were most faithfully and constantly observed, as the reader will easily believe. And in truth, such was his hunger and his desire to receive the most holy Sacrament, that in spite of his habitual maladies, during the forty-five years of his priesthood he never omitted the celebration of the holy sacrifice when he could possibly avoid doing so. Although occasionally unable to stand, and confined to his bed for entire weeks, when the time drew near for him to say Mass, he seemed invested with a supernatural vigor, insomuch that, rising at early dawn, he offered the divine sacrifice with great Fervor. Having ended it, and made a long thanksgiving, he returned to his bed.

His preparation for this holy function lasted about two hours, and he never presented himself at the altar till after a long prayer, a severe discipline, and having purified his heart by sacramental confession, which he frequented daily. The time of his Mass did not usually exceed three quarters of an hour; from time to time, however, he obtained leave of the person who served him to give full vent to his devotion, and then his Mass lasted three or four hours, in a continual ecstasy, with such a flood of tears, sighs, and sobs so vehement, that the server sometimes feared he might rupture a blood vessel and die.

His thanksgiving, which he made kneeling and bare-headed, and when he thought himself secure from observation prostrate with his face upon the ground, was no less fervent, with no other measure of time than that of his own Fervor, being accustomed to say that this was the most proper time to treat with God. With regard to his spending as much time as he could before the Blessed Sacrament, in addition to what has been already said, he was known often to spend whole nights in prayer before it. And as his room was immediately behind the altar, he fixed a little cross on that part of the wall which corresponded with the tabernacle, so that, without going out of his room he turned towards the cross, directing thither his adoration, sighs, and petitions. Moreover, he always passed the recreation hour there, no relief to him being comparable to that. Finally, all his best works, from morning till night, such as prayer, examens, divine office, &c., would not have had the desired savor of devotion if performed elsewhere than at the feet of Jesus in His sacrament of love.

When asked why he did not spare himself, since he might satisfy his devotion in his own room with less inconvenience, he replied, "My Lord Jesus Christ remains shut up in the tabernacle alone; can I do less than go and keep Him company a little?" And when he quitted his dear Lord to attend to his various duties, he never did so without doing violence to himself, saying, "O my Jesus! my body goes away, but I leave my heart here, like the angels who never lose sight of God, even when employed for the benefit of men."

In conclusion, whoever wishes to understand the esteem, love, and exalted sentiments which he entertained towards this most adorable mystery, may consult his "Meditations," and his work "On the perfection of various states of life," in which he handles the subject with an ardent charity, depth of learning, and tenderness of hearty scarcely unworthy of a seraph.

CHAPTER XIX

His tender devotion to our Blessed Lady, his angel-guardian, and to the saints.

O give a correct idea of Father de Ponte's devotion to the most Blessed Virgin, it is but little to say that even from his childhood he had looked upon her as his most beloved Mother, honoring her with such devotions as were compatible with his age, and applying to her in all his necessities. Allusion has already been made to the vow by which he bound himself to defend the doctrine of her Immaculate Conception.

As he advanced in years, and after he became a religious, with a better knowledge and esteem of her dignities, it is incredible how great became his desire to love and serve her more and more. Besides spending a long time every day before her altar, he lost no opportunity of going to offer her his respects, never separating his visits to the Son and to the Mother. Nothing could give him greater pleasure than to introduce a conversation having for its subject her eminent virtues and exalted prerogatives. He spoke of her with such delight and such sublimity as to excite the admiration and tenderness of all who heard him. From her he sought strength and vigor in his labors: he consulted her in all his doubts, and in the decisions he had to make; he had recourse to her for comfort in his maladies and sufferings; finally, she was his refuge, his hope, his every good.

New fuel was added to the beautiful flame of his devotion to Mary by a particular light given him in one of his contemplations on the 117th Psalm, "Open to me the gates of justice: I will go into them, and will give praise to the Lord." We have already referred to this meditation, in which he was given to understand that these gates were the different spiritual helps and means which lead to the knowledge and love of God, and that the first of these was the adorable sacrament of the altar. He was at the same time interiorly taught that the second of these gates is our Blessed Lady and affectionate filial devotion to her, for under this title the Church still salutes her, "Thou art the door of the great King, blessed gate of heaven."

This was quite sufficient to induce him to knock incessantly at this door, and earnestly to beseech this divine Mother to present him to her ever adorable Son, that he might know and love Him with his whole heart. "Oh, what a gate! what a noble gate this is!" he would sometimes say; "blessed are they to whom God opens this gate. It is closed against those who have not a great devotion to Mary, neither can they hope to gain access to the throne of God."

That he might the better deserve her patronage, he let slip no opportunity of honoring her. He daily recited her Rosary, and meditating on its mysteries

OUR LADY AND THE SAINTS

was his sweetest delight; he never omitted this even in illness, or under the most violent spasmodic attacks. Fasting on Saturdays in her honor, and on the vigils of her feasts, was little less than a divine law to him. He prepared himself for her principal solemnities by fervent novenas, longer prayers, and more rigorous austerities. He passed no image or picture of her without respectfully saluting it, and God alone knows how often this occurred every day. He spoke of her whenever he could, both in public and private, endeavoring to excite devotion to her in all hearts. All this, however, did not satisfy his ardent desires, or give sufficient vent to the affection which he had entertained for so beloved a Mother.

As love is ingenious, so did he invent new methods of honoring her. We will instance only one, as characteristic of his insatiable desire to give her pleasure. He undertook to recite her corona daily, but in a particular and sublime manner; inviting, in the first decade, the nine choirs of angels, and especially Saint Gabriel and her guardian angel, to honor her; in the second, the holy patriarchs and prophets, but more expressly Saint Joachim, Saint Anne, and Saint Joseph; in the third, the holy apostles and disciples of our Lord, naming with special devotion Saint John and Saint Luke, as most dear to our Blessed Lady; in the fourth, the numberless martyrs; in the fifth, all the holy confessors and religious of every order; and in the sixth, all the holy virgins and widows, especially those most devoted to her.

But who could explain with what affectionate respect he practiced this beautiful devotion, pausing at every decade, beseeching each class to unite with him in praising their Queen, and in blessing and thanking the divine goodness for having chosen her to be His Mother, and for bestowing on her such signal privileges? He then congratulated with her on her sublime exaltation, and for having so heroically corresponded with the divine intentions; nor did he fail to congratulate also with the angels and saints on their happiness in dwelling forever with her, and enjoying her heavenly affection. Then, turning to the Three Divine Persons, he earnestly entreated Them to make her known throughout the whole world, that she might be loved and esteemed by all mankind. Lastly, he begged her to obtain for him those graces he stood most in need of—power to imitate her virtues, especially her purity and humility. And that he might the more easily secure his petition, he solicited these same angels and saints to be his advocates and mediators with her.

The devotion of the servant of God towards Mary was never more beautifully displayed than in his writings; oh, then it was that he quite surpassed himself. We need only read what he has left us in his commentary on the Book of Canticles, and in his celebrated Meditations, wherein he gives us, as I may say, a compendium of her life. In speaking of her elevated dignity, of the plenitude of her graces, of her divine virtues, of her merits, her prerogatives, and her other endowments, nothing better could be added or desired, so great was his learning, so powerful was his reasoning, so thorough his knowledge of holy Scripture and the Fathers; and above all, his devoted affection and spiritual unction can scarcely be described.

There can be no doubt but that our Blessed Lady, with her accustomed benignity, well repaid her faithful servant by loading him with benefits. It is certain that he ascribed to her whatever there was of good in his soul, and with reason, for we may truly say he was always at her side. In proof of this we will conclude with the narrative of a signal favor conferred by her on this her servant. In one of his contemplations he beheld Jesus Christ nailed to the cross, and our Blessed Lady at the foot of it. Looking at him as He formerly did to Saint John, He said to him, "Dost thou see My most beloved Mother? She must also be thy Mother. Whatever thou wishest of Me have recourse to her, and thou shalt obtain all." Then, turning towards Mary, and pointing to the holy man, He said to her, "My dear Mother, this is thy son; I consign him to thee; show thyself a good Mother to him." At these words our most benign Lady deigned to receive him as such, promising him her protection and her love. We can imagine, but not describe, the happy impression this left on him.

Extraordinary, too, was his devotion to his guardian angel, to whose care God had committed him. He saluted him frequently every day, most gratefully acknowledging his courteous assistance. It was generally believed that his holy angel often visibly appeared to him, and conversed familiarly with him. Next to Mary, he was his most efficacious mediator with God. "Remember," he would say with great confidence, "O my good angel, that I am under your care; it belongs to you to guide, admonish, and reprehend me. Ah! do this for the love you bear my God. Never let me oppose His holy will, and may I always love Him with my whole heart!"

Not less was his devotion to the other angels, especially the archangels Michael and Gabriel; one as the protector of the whole Church, and the other as ambassador of the mystery of the Incarnation. He was also particularly devoted to all those saints who were in any way connected with our Divine Lord, as Saint Joachim, Saint Anne, Saint Joseph, Saint John Baptist, and the Apostles. He had little prints of them in his room, and he used daily to make his stations before them, rejoicing with them for the services they had been able to render to Jesus Christ, and also for the glory which they now enjoy, recommending his soul to them, together with his own necessities and those of others.

CHAPTER XX

Of the supernatural gifts of counsel and discernment of spirits, conferred by God on Father de Ponte, and of his great talent in the direction of souls.

MONGST the many and heroic virtues with which our loving Lord was pleased to adorn the soul of this His faithful servant, one was that of admirable prudence. We may confidently say that it belongs to this virtue to rule and give laws to all the rest. God having chosen him, not merely to be an instrument for the promotion of His glory, but also to give him to the Church as one of the most experienced masters of Christian perfection, and as a distinguished doctor of mystical theology, would furnish his mind with several supernatural and heavenly gifts, amongst which, and in a particular manner, were the gifts of counsel and discernment of spirits, whereby he might easily distinguish true from counterfeit gold, and truth from error. It was thus that God Himself showed him to His chosen servant. Donna Marina di Escobar, who, in one of her visions, saw the holy man completely invested with His Divine Spirit, in the act of learning from Him what he was afterwards to teach others.

Invigorated by this supernatural light, there was no difficulty so intricate, which, as soon as it was proposed to him, he could not dissect, with all its circumstances, treating it with a master's skill, answering in such proper terms, with such solidity of learning, brevity, and clearness, that his solutions were generally looked upon as something miraculous. Continual recourse was had to him from all parts by persons of the highest dignity, ecclesiastic and secular. Archbishops, bishops, ministers of state, and religious of all orders, though learned themselves, consulted him in their doubts with such confidence, "quasi si quis consuleret Deum," to use the Scripture phrase, and never was it known that anyone regretted having followed his advice. This may be understood, not only with regard to spiritual, but also to political affairs which in any manner concerned the divine honor and the salvation of souls. As an instance of this, it will suffice to name Don John Alphonsus Pimentel, Count and Duke of Beneventes, Minister of State, and favorite of the king, who never decided any important negotiation without first consulting Father de Ponte, and this with such satisfaction to himself, that in his juridical deposition on the virtues of the servant of God given after his death, he asserted that he had always found him to be a man of eminent prudence. In proof of this, when the servant of God was asked his opinion with regard to the marriage, almost decided upon, between the Infanta Donna Maria and Charles Prince of Wales, afterwards King of England, although it was approved of by many wise persons, he always said "No," prognosticating great misfortunes if ever it took place. When King Philip III, who highly esteemed the holy man, heard his answer, he immediately broke off the treaty. That his opinion was correct was but too well by the fearful tragedies which soon afterwards occurred in England, of which history gives ample details.

His chief and continual occupation, however, was the culture of souls, guiding them by his counsels in the paths of perfection and salvation. It would be difficult to say how many he assisted, either by replacing them in the right road from which they had deviated, or by enlightening their doubts, or removing their scruples, enlarging their hearts, and restoring their peace of conscience. A few instances will suffice.

A young student felt, in spite of his own heart, a powerful stimulus to enter the Society of Jesus, but the mere idea of abandoning his home and parents threw him into desolation. In order to calm his spirits he asked Father de Ponte's advice, who, compassionating his weakness, affectionately embraced him, saying, "Courage, my son, God will have you here." These few words dispelled all the vain apprehensions and repugnances of the youth. Filled with holy joy, he asked and obtained admission into the Society, where, after laboring much for the service and glory of God, and the good of his neighbor, he died holily.

A lady of the highest nobility in Valladolid was reduced to the greatest misery by the misconduct of her husband, so that even her life was in danger. By way of assuaging her grief a little she went to consult the servant of God, He received her with his usual charity, compassionated and consoled her. After he had advised her how to act, he added, "Lady, the remedy is certainly difficult and distasteful, but if you wish for peace it is necessary." She answered, "You have only to command, father, I am ready." She acted exactly as he prescribed. The consequence was that her husband became even more attached to her than he had formerly been, and they ever after lived in perfect harmony.

There was in the same city a noble young lady, sole heiress of her house, who so anxiously wished to consecrate herself to God in a cloister that she bound herself by vow to do so. In order to destroy this pious wish, her parents engaged her in all the diversions and enjoyments of the world. In a short time the young lady lost her religious vocation, and, as it often happens in such cases, wished to marry. In the meantime her mother died, with feelings of deep remorse for having misled her daughter. The father, doubtful how to act, consulted Father de Ponte on the subject, who, having heard the circumstances, said, "Bring the young lady to me." When she appeared, few were the words of the holy man, but they were weighty, and penetrated as they were intended. "The choice of a state, on which our eternal happiness depends, must be matured with prayer and counsel; it is not to depend upon caprice. Remember your vow, and remember, too, that we may not jest with God. "However," added he, in a tone of authority, "go and place yourself before the Blessed Sacrament, and with utter indifference beseech God to make known to you what He requires of you." To this just and sensible advice the young lady could offer no objection, but, ashamed of herself and her past infidelity, she did as the servant of God desired. In reward of her obedience she heard, during her prayer, a secret interior voice utter these words, "Who can abide in My presence, if they will at the same time dwell in the world and amidst its vanities?" These words completely triumphed over her heart. She soon put on the religious habit, and lived and died with the reputation of no ordinary virtue. Innumerable other instances of this nature might be added which, are omitted for the sake of brevity.

To speak of the discernment of spirits, which, according to the apostle, is a light whereby we distinguish the spiritual man, guided and moved by the Spirit of truth, from him who is not so, although he may appear such. The servant of God may be presumed to have acquired this gift by prayer and contemplation, for he so perfectly understood whatever is comprehended under the name of that profound science, mystical theology, that many persons were of opinion he had clearly expressed, by means of symbols, comparisons, and figures, what previous contemplatives had taught most obscurely. His learning was all the more valuable, as it was not merely a speculative, but a practical knowledge, his own personal experience during a long series of years, supported by assiduous study of holy Scripture and the Fathers. Hence he spoke and wrote on these subjects with such perspicuity and propriety as left nothing more to be desired.

The reader of his works will see that he has furnished the Church with powerful weapons to combat the pernicious errors everywhere disseminated by ancient and modern heretics with such damage to souls as to oblige the vicars of Jesus Christ to fulminate against them the most terrible anathemas. From all that has been hitherto said it will be easy to imagine how cautious he was in the direction of souls, and how circumspect he was in guiding them.

When he met with persons desirous of giving themselves to the exercise of prayer, and of entering upon a more perfect way of life, his first and greatest endeavor was to remove all external display and vain ostentation, to ground them in profound humility and the knowledge of themselves, exacting from them a blind obedience, with a total spoliation of all self-will. He well knew that true sanctity consists in the indefatigable exercise of real solid virtue, such as the interior mortification of the passions, opposing one's own will in all things, in renouncing every delight, and in chastising the body with severe austerities; and this, as he often remarked, was following the path pointed out to us both by the word and example of our Divine Redeemer.

Sometimes our loving Lord treats certain well-disposed souls most dear to Him like a harsh master, drawing them to Himself, it is true, by sublime paths, but very rough and difficult. With such as these Father de Ponte's talent was admirable. He conducted them through every degree of the highest contemplation, preserving them from the snares which the devil made use of in order to deceive them, at the same time suggesting the manner in which they were humbly to receive, and gratefully correspond with, the divine favors which our loving Lord deigned by such ineffable means to confer upon them, admitting them to a more familiar communication with Himself, allowing them to taste the sweets of paradise at the very fountain-head of the Divinity.

These and other celestial gifts bestowed by God on Father de Ponte, and so zealously employed by him to the advantage of innumerable souls which he led to the summit of evangelical perfection, soon gained him such a reputation throughout the Spanish dominions that it was generally thought there was not then living a man more enlightened by God and more intelligent than himself. In fact, the wisest directors applied to him at the first appearance in their penitents of any extraordinary operations, such as visions, ecstasies, raptures, prophecy, and other things found in some persons called to high contemplation. In such cases, where it is doubtful whether these things proceed from a good or evil spirit, (for the devil often clothes himself as an angel of light,) the universal and secure expedient was to refer the matter to Father de Ponte, and leave the decision to him.

In the city of Burgos there was a person who, though reputed spiritual, conducted herself in such a manner as to raise doubts about her and the sincerity of her spirit. The bishop deputed a particular congregation of ecclesiastics and learned religious men to examine the case. After many meetings it still remained obscure; opinions were divided, when, at last, by common consent, a man was dispatched to Valladolid, with the requisite informations, to Father de Ponte, as to an oracle, remitting the whole to his decision. His answer was accepted by all parties, even by those who had been of a contrary opinion.

The Bishop of Avila had, in one of his monasteries, a religious named Donna Maria Vela, whom God had guided by so difficult a path, so interlaced with thorns, that not only her companions, but even superiors themselves, knew not how to decide, or from what spirit many of her actions proceeded. One thing she did was to observe a total fast on the days of her communion, and on the day following it she felt stronger and in better health than before it. On the contrary, if compelled by obedience to eat on that day, she experienced such convulsions of the stomach as obliged her violently to reject what she had swallowed. Father de Ponte was requested to examine her, and after trying her in various ways, he approved her spirit as good and proceeding from God. However, to put an end to murmurs and divisions in the community on her account, he ordered her to fast on communion days only as she would fast in Lent. The religious immediately obeyed, and was left to live in peace, those who had been most incredulous loving and esteeming her ever after. She acquired a high reputation for sanctity, and her Life is preparing for the press.

In another town a young religious was favored by God with extraordinary gifts, and as they appeared exteriorly, much confusion was caused in the community, diversity of opinion arising as to what spirit guided her. Being examined by the servant of God, who subjected her to various trials, he decided that she was led by the Spirit of God; but with great prudence desired her to lay aside whatever appeared externally, since it was an occasion of dissension. The nun declared herself unable to do this, having no control over the matter. The holy man answered her, "Yes, yes, you can; however, supposing it to be beyond your power, beseech your Spouse to remove the

DISCERNMENT OF SPIRITS 163

difficulty." She obeyed, and was immediately heard. All litigation ceased, and she quietly advanced in the paths of sanctity.

In the convent of S. Austin, at Valladolid, there was a religious who felt such a repugnance when approaching to receive holy communion, that it seemed almost to equal the pains of death. A religious man of another order, who heard her confessions, judged this to be the work of the devil, and recommended exorcism to cure her. However, he advised her to consult Father de Ponte, a holy man of great experience, and much enlightened in such affairs. The servant of God being called, tried her in many ways, after which he said to her, "Daughter, have courage, fear not; this is not the work of the devil, nor is there any need of exorcisms. It is a cross which your Divine Spouse sends you; carry it willingly. Henceforth, before you approach to receive Him, say to Him with sincerity of heart, 'Lord, what I suffer, I suffer willingly for You.' And then, if it seems to you that you are distracted, communicate nevertheless, this being the road whereby you are to reach salvation." The nun obeyed, and in reward of her obedience her good God soon afterwards freed her from her trial.

In the monastery of the Holy Ghost, at Olmedo, were three religious who aimed at perfection, it is true, but by means so uncommon as not to be understood by the generality of men. They were under the jurisdiction of the Bishop of Avila, who suffered much anxiety on their account. Many, believing them deluded by the devil, were of opinion that they ought to be denounced before the tribunal of the holy inquisition. Father de Ponte hearing this, begged to be minutely informed of all that concerned them, and their manner of life, after which he concluded that two of them were led by a good spirit. As for the third, he looked upon her as a silly woman, —not bad, but foolish. This decision was fully approved of by the inquisition.

I shall conclude this chapter with two short reflections found amongst the writings of the author of his Life in Spanish, who was co-temporary with him. The first is, that of all those persons (and they were many) whose extraordinary mode of life was, according to his opinion, the result of a good spirit, not one of them was afterwards proved to be either deceiving or deceived. The other is, that so long as the holy man lived, there was no person, so to speak, of distinguished virtue throughout Spain, who felt secure of being in the path of perfection unless they had, by word of mouth or writing, his assurance to that effect.

CHAPTER XXI

Prophecies of Father de Ponte, and other gifts conferred on him by God.

LTHOUGH prophecy, according to the teaching of Saint Gregory, is, strictly speaking, a manifestation of future events known only to God,—"Show the things that are to come hereafter, and we shall know that ye are gods,"—in its more ample signification it means a knowledge of present and future things, which, owing to distance of time and place, or in any other manner hidden to us, could not possibly be known to us by mere natural light. In this its extended sense God conferred the gift on Father de Ponte, as the following incidents will clearly show.

Donna Catherine di Osorio, a noble young lady of Valladolid, was called by God to the order of the Discalced Carmelites. Her parents did not so much oppose her being a nun, but they objected to the institute of her choice. They said so much to dissuade her from her purpose, that, overcome by the respect due to them, she changed her mind, and joined a very different institute, in the convent of the Holy Ghost. What was the consequence? In place of the peace which she had hoped to find, her mind became a prey to the deepest uneasiness. However regular that community might be, she was not in the place where God would have her. To calm the tempest in her soul, she asked and obtained leave to consult Father de Ponte, of whom she had heard so much. Having listened to the account of herself and her agitations, he said to her, "Daughter, be consoled, and rest assured that notwithstanding all the difficulties which at present seem insurmountable, a year will not pass over ere your desires are accomplished, and you will join the Discalced in the convent called the Laura; in the meantime arm yourself with patience, and faithfully comply with your exercises of piety." As the servant of God predicted, so it happened; and after his death the nun declared on oath that she had ever considered this to have been a most certain prophecy.

A Castilian nobleman, calling to visit the father, related a wonderful escape from danger as he was traveling on horseback. "My lord," rejoined the holy man, "I rejoice exceedingly, and heartily thank God; but be more careful of yourself, and guard against another danger, which will not end as this has done." Several persons heard the caution, and looked upon it as prophetical. In effect it was soon verified, for a few days later, as the nobleman was riding, wishing to take a leap, he was violently thrown off the saddle, and died before assistance could be procured.

Mother Angela of the Incarnation, an Augustinian nun of Valladolid, attested on oath that whilst yet a secular, and a mere girl, she consulted Father de Ponte on the subject of her vocation. Having approved it, he added, "Provide yourself in time with a stock of solid virtue, especially with great patience, because in a few years you will experience great troubles and temptations." He gave her directions also how to conduct herself under them. Everything occurred exactly as he had foretold, and she acknowledged herself much benefitted by the instructions she then received from the servant of God.

Whilst Father Girolamo di Tobar was in the noviciate at Villa-Garcia, Father de Ponte one day said to him, "Brother, after long labor in the service of religion you will end your days in this house." Some years later Father Girolamo fell dangerously ill in the college of Monterei, when the doctors gave up all hopes of saving him. He himself, however, positively asserted that he should not die either of that illness, or in that town, saying that the saintly Father de Ponte had prophesied the contrary; and, in fact, he recovered. When grown old he was sent to Villa-Garcia, where he met with the same infirmarian that had nursed him at Monterei, who at once said to him, "Is your reverence come here to die? Such was foretold you by Father de Ponte, was it not?" He answered, "Yes, exactly so, and the prediction will soon be verified." And so it was, for not long afterwards he fell ill. Worn out by labor, and laden with merit, he closed his holy life by a holy death.

A person, whose name is not recorded, was grievously offended by a young nobleman; engaging the assistance of several assassins he resolved to sacrifice him to his vengeance. The other, being apprized of his danger, armed himself in his own defense, to the unspeakable anxiety of his parents, who trembled at their son's danger; to preserve him from it they implored the prayers and counsels of Father de Ponte, who said to them, "No, fear not, the offended person will abandon all attempt against your son's life, and from this moment renounces every feeling of bitterness." Then, sending for the young man, he said to him, "My lord, take my advice, lay aside your arms." The other interrupted him with, "Father, what are you saying? My life is in question; the person I have offended insists upon my death, cost what it may. Have I no need of precaution, then?" "Have no doubt," rejoined the holy man, "of what I now assure you; no evil will befall you." He could have known this only by divine revelation, for everything tended to show the contrary. The nobleman, however, obeyed, and Father de Ponte's prediction proved strictly true. Most persons attributed to his prayers the fact of the offended party giving up all idea of revenge, without so much as having sought satisfaction for the offence.

The licentiate Zebaglios, a physician, and one of Father de Ponte's penitents, whilst in conversation with him, was asked whether he had courage enough to bear a quartan fever? "Yes, why not?" replied the doctor; but here the subject dropped. A few days later, Zebaglios found himself really attacked by the said quartan fever. He was astonished at the circumstance, and on one of the days when free from the paroxysm, he went off to Father de Ponte, who at once accosted him with, "Well, Signor! how goes on the quartan fever?" "Ah! my dear Father! it treats me very ill indeed." "Come, come," replied the holy man, "be of good heart, the fever will return no more." Nor did it return, and the sick man was perfectly cured.

Being aware that in the convent of the Incarnation there was a novice who mingled childish levity even in her exercises of piety. He thus addressed himself to God: "O my God! this is far otherwise than I could wish. This young person will one day be the superior of this community: these two things are quite incompatible." The result was, that as the novice advanced in age she became steady; in fact, a person of solid virtue; she afterwards governed the community to the great advantage of regular observance, and died deeply regretted by her religious sisters.

During the years that the holy man was superior, it was generally believed that he saw the interior of his subjects; and by a supernatural light, could, when in his room, or before the Blessed Sacrament, or visiting the sick in the infirmary, tell what was passing in the most secret corners of the house. And this belief contributed not a little to keep people in due subjection. In the college of S. Ambrose, Father Ludovico Valdivia once went very early to Father de Ponte's room, wishing to confer with him on some secret matters of conscience; before he could open his lips, the holy man began, and showed him that he knew perfectly well all that was weighing on his mind; for which he gave him the most suitable remedies, and then said to him, "Father Valdivia, we shall be able to converse more conveniently some other time; I am occupied just at present." But he, having found what he wanted, went away exclaiming, "Oh what a saint! what a saint!"

It was remarked by many, that in his visits to the sick, whenever the servant of God told them not to fear, but to have full hope, they always recovered; but when, on the contrary, he exhorted them to place themselves in the hands of God, and to be resigned to His holy will, they always died.

Donna Maddalena Cisneros, of Valladolid, declared on oath that the servant of God had manifested to her in confession some of her most hidden sins, which she had never revealed to anyone.

Don Alfonso Pimentel, Count and Duke of Beneventes, Don James Gomez di Sandoval, Count of Saldagna, and Don Giacomo di S. Stefano, Marquis of Olivares, three grandees of the first class, all much loved by the king of Spain, attested on oath, that consulting Father de Ponte at various times on most important affairs, he knew beforehand what they wished to say to him, and gave the answers with his usual prudence and judgment.

Lastly, Don Antonio Valbon Mongrobejo, many years his penitent, thus gave his deposition: "Through him I succeeded in my affairs and occupations; was extricated from many trials and difficulties, which otherwise 1 should not have escaped, he always foretelling me what was going to happen, and predicting many things which were afterwards literally accomplished."

We might never finish our account of the celestial gifts bestowed on him by God, if we undertook to relate all. Frequent were his ecstasies, visions, sublime intelligences, wonderful splendor, dominion over devils, and over nature itself; all ornaments with which God is accustomed to adorn His servants, when He intends to evidence them to the world. Whether he prayed before the Blessed Sacrament, or celebrated holy mass, or in whatever other manner he held communication with our Lord, a sweet ecstasy soon raised him towards his Sovereign Good, and this with so much impetuosity, that his soul, drawing his body with it, often raised him to a considerable distance from the ground.

In some of the many visions by which he was admitted to a more familiar communication with God, a sublime intelligence was given him with regard to the Divine attributes, the most sacred mysteries of human redemption, and of the state of souls; God conversing with him as one friend would with another. Of these visions some few have reached us written with his own hand, and from them we may guess what the others must have been, which were known only to God and himself.

In the colleges where he lived, it was looked upon as a certain thing that his angel-guardian and other angels conversed familiarly with him. Words which occasionally slipped from him unawares, and several other indications, confirmed this belief. Donna Marina di Escobar declared on oath, that God had allowed her to see those blessed spirits in the act of comforting the holy man with heavenly balsams, when he was suffering under his heavy infirmities and weakness. A supernatural resplendent light was seen, sometimes like a globe suspended above his head, sometimes in rays surrounding his face, and sometimes so distended as to invest his whole person; this is asserted by several ocular witnesses. I will here add the words of Father Alegambe, in his "Catalogue of the Writers of the Society;" when speaking of Father de Ponte, he says, "He was often seen with bright rays encircling his body. Sometimes a globe of the most effulgent light appeared above his head, at other times he seemed to send forth rays of light from his whole body, he himself being wholly encircled with them; his very room shaking, and the timbers of the room creaking."

How great his power was over the devils, the very fiends confessed in spite of themselves. One day Donna Marina di Escobar lay on her poor little bed, suffering the most excruciating pain. As soon as the holy man was aware of it, he went as usual to console and instruct her. A supernatural light, which never abandoned him, enabled him at once to see that her suffering was caused by the devil. In an imperious tone he commanded the malignant spirit to depart immediately, and to molest the sick woman no more. This was quite enough; the terrified fiend instantly fled, and Donna Marina's tortures ceased. In her juridical deposition, after attesting this fact, she added that she had seen and heard the devils in a fury revile the holy man, exclaiming, "Accursed be that old man who opposes us in everything, and defeats all our schemes!"

In speaking of the miraculous favors granted by God to the merits of His servant during his life-time, we may say that he was himself the greatest miracle; applying to him what S. Bernard wrote of the holy bishop, S. Malachy: "Primum et maximum miraculorum quod fecit, ipse erat." Several doctors declared on oath, that considering his extreme weakness, and the emaciated state of his body, they believed him to live by miracle, and every action of his to be a prodigy; since he had not the ordinary dispositions essential to life. The same was asserted by other persons; a life could not be otherwise than miraculous, which allowed such continual labor and fatigue, under such an accumulation of infirmities and suffering. On one occasion the fathers of the college entreated the doctor to check the harassing sort of life which the servant of God was pursuing; he answered, "My dear Father, we must leave Father de Ponte to go on his own way, for he has another and superior Physician, who preserves his life, and supplies him with strength to work."

However austere and inexorable he was to himself, refusing his body all relief, still he was compassionate towards others, feeling their trials more than his own; and he only wished to have influence with God, that he might be able to help them. We will give a few proofs taken from the process begun for his canonization.

Donna Isabella de Mercado, a very pious lady of Valladolid, and a penitent of his, was attacked by a violent fever, accompanied with excruciating pain in one ear and eye; her throat was so swollen that she could swallow nothing: bleeding had afforded her no relief, and the doctors considered her life in great danger. In this state of affairs the holy man went to visit her; entering her room, and seeing her thus oppressed, he said to her, "And what is the matter now? What complaint afflicts you, lady?" "My dearest Father," replied she, "God has ordained this for my sins, and has not allowed me to receive Him this morning." It was a day on which she usually communicated. "Come, come," said he, "be consoled, and be of good heart; the same Lord that bound you knows how to liberate you.'" Wonderful to relate, scarcely had the holy man uttered these words, when the lady was perfectly cured. She arose from her bed that very morning, went to the church, communicated, and assisted at all the other holy functions there.

We have already alluded to an instance of the same nature, when speaking of his charity towards his neighbor.

Whilst Father Francis Ribera was in the college at Villa-Garcia, he was suddenly seized one morning with a violent pain; and according to the opinion of the doctors, was at the point of death. Father de Ponte was then rector, and hastened to him, when he found him delirious, and the malady at its utmost height; he did nothing more than place his hand upon the sick man's head, reciting at the same time a gospel over him, when the pain instantaneously ceased, and he was perfectly cured.

Mother Mary of the Holy Ghost, prioress of the Augustinian convent at Valladolid, was confined to her bed by a violent attack of sciatica, and was at the same time oppressed with great interior affliction and anguish. To give some little vent to her distress, she applied by note to Father de Ponte. By way of answer, he sent her in writing some devout prayer, exhorting her to recite it with a lively faith. She obeyed, and to the surprise of everyone was immediately cured both in mind and body.

The following case was deposed on oath by the doctor Zebaglios, of whom mention has already been made; we cite his own words: "Whilst Father de Ponte was still living I was once in great interior affliction concerning an affair of the highest importance. I began to pray, beseeching the Divine Majesty to grant my petition in consideration of the merits of my saintly Father de Ponte. All in a moment I clearly saw before me the servant of God ill upon his poor little bed, who began to reason with me; my heart was immediately relieved, and my soul was restored to perfect peace. I have every reason to believe that this was either an imaginary vision, proceeding from God; or a still greater miracle, in which, by divine power, the holy man was endowed with the gift of bilocation."

A young religious went one morning to Father de Ponte, and asked leave to go to bed, saying that he felt ill. The servant of God looked earnestly at him, and with much compassion affectionately embraced him, adding these words, "Yes, my son I but confess first, and dispose yourself to receive the holy viaticum, for our good God will have you with Himself and you have now but a few hours to live." The youth received the intelligence with Christian resignation, begged the father in charity to assist him in that fearful passage, prepared himself with all the Fervor of his heart, received all the rites of the Church, and a few hours later died in the arms of his holy superior. But it is now time to contemplate the death of the holy man himself, who, laden with years and merits, sighed for nothing more than to fly and rest in the bosom of his God.

CHAPTER XXII

His holy death, and its attendant circumstances.

THE servant of God had now entered upon the year 1624, being seventy years of age; and though being reduced by illness to a mere living skeleton, whose very life the doctors held to be miraculous, he nevertheless vanquished his natural weakness by the vigor of his mind, incessantly employing himself either in study or in hearing confessions. From various indications many began to suspect that he had not long to live: it was even thought he had been admonished by God to that effect. He seemed unable to speak of anything but his approaching death, frequently repeating, "The time of my dissolution is at hand." From time to time he was seen with his eyes fixed on heaven, giving way to transports of joy, like unto one who, after a long and tempestuous navigation, finds himself in sight of a port. At other times, on the contrary, he was seized with dreadful fear of being called to give an account of himself, when, throwing himself on his knees before a crucifix, with bitter tears he would exclaim, "When Thou comest to judgment, O Lord, condemn me not."

The impression about his death was much

strengthened one morning, (about a fortnight before it occurred,) when he sent for his confessor. Father Pietro di Sandoval, and requested him to hear his general confession. "Very willingly," replied the other; "but what new idea is this? Thanks be to God, your reverence's health is not worse than it has been for some months past." "I know and am certain," said the holy man, "that the time of my dissolution is at hand." He made his confession with such compunction and such floods of tears as to compel his confessor to weep with him. This is usual with saints, who weigh even the least defects in the scales of the sanctuary, and not in those of this deceitful world. Neither could he be satisfied on the following day until he had received his dear Lord by way of viaticum. The Blessed Sacrament had ever been the chief object of his love, and before it, it may truly be said, he had spent the greater part of his life.

Consoled with this divine food and true bread of the strong, it is easy to guess how he employed the short remnant of life yet allotted to him.

When charity did not call him to the service of his neighbor he was usually alone, attending solely to his preparation for the grand journey soon to be undertaken. When it became known in the town that the holy man's death was at hand, prelates, princes, and all his penitents hastened to confess to him, to put in order their consciences, and to receive his last instructions. He could refuse himself to no one, but welcomed all with charity and cheerfulness, and satisfied them all.

When they expressed their concern and affliction at the prospect of losing him, he with a smiling countenance said to them, "My children, why are you sorrowful? The Master calls, it becomes me to answer. Yes, let us go to Him: the time of my dissolution is at hand. You in the meantime remain true to God, continue to serve Him faithfully, and fear not. He deserves this; He is a good pay-master. As for me, be assured I carry you all in my heart, and if our Lord mercifully admits me amongst the elect, I will not be unmindful of you."

Matters rested thus till the sixteenth day of February, the last of his life; yet no one could believe his death to be so near, though he himself so positively asserted it. The doctors said he had no fever, and that his debility, similar to what it had been for some months past, gave no sign of immediate dissolution; on the contrary, the weakness of his chest seemed better. Many were confirmed in this belief by seeing him on that very day employ five or six hours in dictating various things, and putting a last hand to what he had written about his celebrated penitent, Donna Marina di Escobar. This had been the work of thirty-two years, and at a later period contributed much to the glory of God. But whatever others might think, he never lost sight of his immediate death, and spoke of it with so much certainty, that when someone offered him a glass of jelly, he said, "Oh, before this glass is empty I shall have ceased to live." Then he asked what time it was, and being informed, he added, "Yes, so it is; there is still time." And without saying more, he resumed his sweet colloquies with his loving Lord. And here we may refer to a circumstance which caused great surprise, but which may now serve as an important lesson to us, namely, that a man held in such high repute for sanctity, whose sole aim had ever been to please God and accomplish His holy will, should repute himself the greatest of sinners, and with fear and trembling have no prayer more frequently in his mouth and heart than this: "Lord, when Thou comest to judgment, condemn me not." So great is the terror, even of the saints, at the thought of soon appearing at the tribunal of Christ their Judge.

But the day was on the wane without any mention of Extreme Unction. He, therefore, turning to those who assisted him, said, "Since the doctor is not yet come, beseech Father Rector not to defer this consolation whilst there is still time." At this request the superior was perplexed how best to act, when the doctor most opportunely arrived, who, though he found his pulse but very little weaker, yielded to the earnest and humble entreaties of the sick man, by consenting to the administration of the sacrament. He received it with those sentiments of tender devotion as might well be expected from him. With the same dispositions of soul he attended to the last recommendation, (recited at his own request,) answering all the prayers with great presence of mind and Fervor of heart, moving all the assistants to tears of devotion. He then asked as a favor to be left some time alone.

For two whole hours did the holy man remain immoveable in profound silence, like one in a deep sleep. But in truth his was no sleep, but one of those raptures so familiar to him, wherein the soul, wholly immersed in God and in the contemplation of heavenly things, forgets the body, and in a manner

HIS HOLY DEATH

loses the use of its senses. That such was his case was evident from the starts, the extraordinary appearance of his face, the deep sighs, the sweet tears, the tender manner in which he repeatedly kissed the sacred wounds of his crucified Lord.

They had already reached the fifth hour of the night without any sign of immediate death, therefore they all retired to rest. But they were mistaken. When the sick man was offered some restorative, he replied in a languid voice, "No, there is no more time for that." The superior, being informed of it, gave notice to all the community, everyone wishing to be present at his happy transit. His room was soon filled with his religious brethren, who earnestly asked him to give them a last instruction, but his humility could not consent to this. He frequently repeated these words: "Lord, when Thou comest to judgment condemn me not." He asked by signs for the blessed candle, and holding it in his hand in protestation of his faith, he cast a last loving look on his crucified Lord, and with these words, "Lord, into Thy hands I commend my spirit," he calmly expired on the 16th of February, 1624, having completed his seventieth year. On a Friday, about the middle of the night, he went to receive the reward of his many and heroic virtues.

Amongst many others, it was revealed to the venerable servant of God, Marina di Escobar, that his blessed soul, accompanied by innumerable angels who had assisted at his death, proceeded direct to heaven, without passing through purgatory. She herself declared on oath that she had been allowed to see the holy man at the moment of death invested with glory, having on his breast the holy name of Jesus, resplendent with such brilliant rays of light as quite to eclipse the sun. Nor did this happen once only; he visited her several times, either to instruct her in her doubts, or comfort her in her sufferings, assuring her, moreover, that it was the will of God that he should continue, even from heaven, to be her director and her master.

With regard to his venerated body, there were several circumstances which even the doctors considered miraculous. 1. Though the holy man died in the severest season of the year, whilst snow abounded, and although the cold had almost benumbed him when alive, yet the body remained for a long time soft and flexible. The second was, that whereas in life he had been of dark complexion, and so thin as to resemble a skull covered with skin, when dead, to the astonishment of everyone, his face became plump and fairer than it had ever been, even in his youth. 3. Whilst dead bodies naturally inspire horror and fear, that of the holy man moved all who beheld it to devotion. 4. On hearing of the death of the servant of God, those who had most loved him in life, and who most bitterly deplored his loss, instead of feeling inclined to assist his soul with their prayers, were interiorly pressed and in a manner compelled to recommend themselves to him, and implore his protection before God. To this we may add what the so frequently-named servant of God, Marina di Escobar, knew by revelation, viz., that a numerous company of angels, after having assisted at his happy death, and accompanied his soul to heaven, continued during the remainder of that night and following day to keep watch round the venerated corpse, their brilliant splendor changing the room of the deceased into a little paradise.

No sooner was it known that Father de Ponte had passed to a better life, than great numbers of religious and seculars, notwithstanding the rigorous season, hastened to the college, earnestly entreating to see him once again, though dead, and kiss his feet and hands. Many painters wished to take his portrait; whilst other pious persons suggested that his Life should be written for the comfort and example of posterity; everyone, in fine, strove to show his esteem, love, and devotion, towards such a man. When the corpse was conveyed into the church for the funeral obsequies, as is customary in the Society, it was deemed advisable, in order to avoid tumult, to limit the admissions to such only as were invited. But how could that be kept quiet which was known to so many people? Scarcely was the office of the dead commenced, when not only was the church completely filled, but the crowd, always indiscreet, even in its devotion, broke down the barriers, surrounded the bier, one kissed his hands and feet, others touched him with their beads; some cut his hair, his garments, and would not even have spared his flesh, if the assistants had not by main force and with much difficulty withdrawn the body into the sacristy, inclosing it immediately in a coffin, which, when the doors of the church were closed, was buried at the gospel-side of the altar.

When the news became public, many of the most distinguished nobles, amongst others the Count Duke of Beneventes, the Duchess of Medina di Rio Secco, the Countess Miranda, and many more, formerly his penitents, amicably quarreled with us for not having been informed of his dangerous illness and death; at the same time earnestly begging to have some little thing that had belonged to him, to keep as a precious relic; and so many required this, that the vestments he had used for the celebration of the holy sacrifice, and some others of his garments, when cut up into very small pieces did not suffice to satisfy all.

On the octave day of his death, the religious of Saint Dominic, from whom the servant of God had first imbibed the milk of piety, and for whom he had always entertained the highest esteem and love, repaired in a body to our church of S. Ambrose, there to celebrate the solemn obsequies. The city, too, chose the church of S. Ignatius as the most spacious; and in attestation of its gratitude for the services rendered to it by the holy man, had a sumptuous funeral, with solemn mass and a funeral oration, which was attended by the lords and ministers of the royal auditory, the nobility, and all the most distinguished citizens.

So numerous and wonderful were the favors which the holy man daily obtained for those who had recourse to him, as to excite a general desire that the venerated corpse should be more respectfully lodged, and have a suitable inscription placed over it. Consequently, the year following, 1625, on the 18th of September, he was exhumed, and the coffin opened: the body was found half decayed, yet so that he could be recognized by those who were present. His brain alone remained perfect, as fresh, soft, and well-colored, as if he had died the previous day. It was wonderful that the body, though half putrefied, should yet emit no unpleasant odor; on the contrary, it exhaled a certain sweetness pleasing to all; particularly observed by the three doctors called to be present at the recognition of the body, who declared that this could not be natural. The bishop of the city, with other prelates and religious, would be eye-witnesses of the above related facts. He then ordered three of our priests to swear to the identity of the body, which was inclosed anew in the case and sealed; a public and authentic document was drawn up by notaries, conformably to the decrees relating to such matters: it was then restored to its former place, and the following inscription was placed over it: "Here rests the body of the venerable Father Louis de Ponte, of the Society of Jesus, who died on the 16th of February, 1624."

The number of miracles performed by the holy man in favor of his devout clients continuing to increase, many of our religious, as well as the whole city of Valladolid, besought the Bishop, Monsignor Alfonso Lopez Gallo, to allow a juridical examination and process to be instituted. At the same time the city and college presented a memorial to his most Catholic Majesty Philip IV, beseeching him to obtain from the Sovereign Pontiff the privilege of publicly honoring the servant of God. But various obstacles then prevented its execution; and it was only in 1759 that the necessary examinations and discussions of the cause in the various congregations, according to the usages of Rome, and before the Sovereign Pontiff Clement XIII, were completed. On the 16th of July, that same year 1759, the apostolic see issued the decree, "Constare de virtutibus in gradu heroico tum

Theologalibus, Fide, Spe et Charitate erga Deum, et proximum, quam Cardinalibus, Prudentia, Justitia, Fortitudine et Temperantia Ven. Servi Dei Ludovici a Ponte Sacerdotis Professi Societatis Jesu, in casu et ad effectum de quo agitur." It is in virtue of this decree that the servant of God is styled Venerable.

CHAPTER XXIII

Miracles performed by God through the merits of his servant, after his death.

UR Divine and loving Lord, who had so liberally enriched Father de Ponte in life with such illustrious gifts, would also accredit his sanctity, by granting undeniable miracles to his merits and intercession after his death. Of these miracles many are reported in the authentic processes for his canonization; many others are related by those who in their greatest necessities had recourse to his intercession, and who experienced it in a manner evidently miraculous. A few only will be introduced here, of those in which God was pleased to manifest His will that this His servant should be glorified on earth; showing too, at the same time, the benevolence of the holy man in attending, now that he is in heaven, to the welfare of those who with faith and confidence implore his patronage.

Donna Catarina della Valle, wife of Don Girolamo Avellenado, being already in delicate health, was attacked with a violent fever. Several physicians were consulted, all remedies applied, but without success;

on the contrary, the malady gained strength daily, so much so, that the lady received the viaticum. Whilst she was in this deplorable state someone advised her to have recourse to the Venerable Father de Ponte, who was daily bestowing such great favors on those who implored his aid. Hearing this, she felt great hope of recovering her health through his means, and in case she did, she bound herself by vow to visit the chapel where he was entombed, and hear Mass there, as soon as she should be able to leave the house, and also to recite several devout prayers in his honor. Then, taking up a picture of him, she respectfully kissed it, and applied it to the part where she was suffering most pain. The moment she did this she found herself surprisingly relieved; in fact, she was rescued, as we may say, from the jaws of death. A few days later she was in perfect health, and gladly acquitted herself of her vow.

Donna Maddalena de Cisneros, descending a staircase in her own house, missed the first step, and was violently precipitated from the top to the bottom, head foremost. She must inevitably have been killed had she not, whilst in the very act of falling, recommended herself most devoutly to the Venerable Father de Ponte, and invoked his help. Her call was not in vain, for, to the astonishment of those who hastened to her assistance, and who expected, at the least, to find her with broken bones, they had the satisfaction to see her standing on her feet at the bottom of the staircase, not only uninjured, but even undismayed. After returning most humble thanks to her deliverer she pursued her walk.

In 1624 a nobleman, named Don Clemente

MIRACLES

Formento, governor of Valladolid, fell ill of a malignant spotted fever. Recourse was had to every remedy, but the malady soon overspread his whole body, and was carrying him rapidly to the grave. As a last resource Father de Ponte was appealed to. A picture of him was procured, which the sick man applied several times, blessing himself with it, and earnestly beseeching the holy man to obtain the restoration of his health. At first he really seemed better, and the complaint was thought to be yielding; but suddenly another change for the worse ensued. The last sacraments were hastily administered. He was reduced to the last extremity, had lost all sense; the recommendation of the soul and other prayers of the Church had been recited, and his last sigh was momentarily expected; in fact, the habit of S. Francis, in which he had expressed a wish to be buried, was actually prepared for him.

But the servant of God appears only to have deferred his assistance, to make the cure more wonderful, and to confer something beyond the one favor asked. The disconsolate wife and children, together with their surrounding friends, again had recourse to the holy man, and again blessed the sufferer with the picture, when he immediately opened his eyes, recovered his senses, and, contrary to all expectation, visibly improved, so much so, that in a few days no vestige of the malady remained, and he was perfectly cured. He then proceeded to the father's tomb, and whilst he was in the act of thanking him for thus being delivered from the fangs of death, he seemed to see the holy man, who with a grave and cheerful countenance said to him, "I have obtained for you more than you asked." From that time Clemente constantly wore the same little picture about his person, and years afterwards protested that in all his necessities the father had ever shown himself propitious to him.

Whilst Father Joseph Cavello was residing at Leon, in Spain, he became possessed of a small particle of Father de Ponte's bone, which he highly valued, and that it might be the more respectfully preserved he consigned it to a silversmith named Pietro de Miranda, desiring him to enclose it in a little crystal column, with a pedestal and capital, both to be of silver. The case being completed, nothing remained to be done but to adjust the bone within the crystal, shut and fasten it. The artificer did not know that it was a bone of Father de Ponte's, but was surprised, as he was trying to fix it in its place, to see it distill several drops of fine fluid. Not suspecting the mystery, he attempted to wipe both the bone and column two or three times, but to no purpose; the liquid was only more copious than before. He suspended the work, carefully folding up in separate papers the bone, the crystal, and the silver, locking all up in a trunk, putting the key in his own pocket. Some days afterwards he was going to resume his work, when, to his utter surprise, he found the bone secured in the reliquary, the column fixed on the pedestal, and the summit covered and fast; in fact, there was nothing left for him to do. His fellow-workman, like himself, was an eye-witness of the fact, and both considered it to be a real miracle, in which opinion they were strongly confirmed, as from day to day they heard of the many prodigies wrought by the holy man.

MIRACLES

For nearly twenty years Donna Maria Quignones, Marchioness de los Veles, had suffered from an oppression of the chest, which, amongst other alarming symptoms, so completely overpowered her as almost to produce suffocation. Remedies only seemed to increase the evil; frequent bleedings afforded no relief. One night, when she felt unusually oppressed and unable to sleep, she recollected that she had a small piece of an amice used by Father de Ponte in offering the holy Mass, and which as a great favor had been given to her. She kissed it repeatedly with great tenderness and respect, placed it upon her chest, and with earnest tears implored his aid. What cannot humble prayer and lively faith accomplish? At that very moment the pain ceased, the complaint disappeared, and she was perfectly cured, enjoying good health for many years.

Antonio della Valle, a child of four years old, son of one of the auditors of the cancellaria, accidentally picked up the buckle of a girdle, and began to play with it, but at length incautiously put it in his mouth and attempted to swallow it. It remained fixed in his throat, and threatened almost immediate death. His face became black, his eyes were swollen, and started from their sockets. The screams of the child aroused his mother, who was sleeping in an adjoining room. Terrified at the awful appearance of her son, she hastily placed a small particle of the bone of Father de Ponte, (which she was fortunate enough to have in the house,) in the mouth of the dying boy. The prodigy was instantaneous; he spoke, saying that the buckle was swallowed, having descended as low as the stomach. His natural color returned, and his eyes resumed their due place and proportions. The buckle, however, remained in the child's body, and caused some alarm lest it might produce laceration of the intestines; but at the end of three days it was ejected without occasioning any pain to the child, who was thus completely cured.

In 1659 a nun, named Donna Francesca di Ribera, of the order of S. Bernard, at Valladolid, had obtained a letter in Father de Ponte's own writing. From esteem of him, and a desire to secure his favor, she always wore this letter upon her, for which purpose she had stitched it in her habit, between the lining and the material itself. At the beginning of the summer she sent this habit to the wash, without a moment's thought of the letter tacked within it. It was soon plunged into hot water, well rubbed with soap, twisted and re-twisted, as is usual in washing, and was in due time returned to the religious, who at the approach of winter again intended to resume her habit. Then it was that she remembered her letter, and in grief of heart exclaimed, "O God! my letter must surely have been utterly destroyed by the washerwoman!" She immediately began to unstitch the habit, when, to her astonishment and delight, she found her letter not only without fracture, but quite perfect, the writing uninjured, and altogether in a better condition than before the accident. Everyone cried out, "A miracle! a miracle!" and in truth it was a miracle, and a great one too; for the same experiment being tried on other letters and papers, they were soon reduced to a mere mass of pulp. The consequence was, the letter of the servant of God was most respectfully lodged, and considered a very precious relic.

MIRACLES

Donna Antonia Maria di Cordova, Marchioness of Villa, had a cross given to her which Father de Ponte had been in the habit of wearing. She declared on oath that she had found in it relief under all her illnesses and trials. These are her words: "In my infirmities and sufferings I had recourse to the intercession of the Venerable Father Louis de Ponte, applying the cross which he himself had worn, and my sufferings were immediately relieved. I did the same, and with the same success, to my children in their different illnesses." So far the lady.

Don Ludovico Blanco, a nobleman of Valladolid, suffered most excruciating pain in consequence of a dangerous obstruction. No remedy afforded any relief, and he was evidently near death, when, recollecting that his wife had obtained many miraculous favors by means of a picture and signature of Father de Ponte's, he had recourse to the same, blessing, and signing himself with them several times, beseeching the Divine Majesty to mitigate his atrocious spasms, and restore him to health, through the merits of His faithful servant. Before the expiration of a quarter of an hour the obstruction yielded, and immediate relief was the consequence. In the opinion of the doctors this was an evident miracle, the invalid having ejected two fleshy substances, one the size of a hazel-nut, the other of a pea, which they declared could not naturally have occurred. He was at the same time perfectly cured, and never after suffered from anything of that description.

We will close this subject, and with it this history, by quoting a passage found in a manuscript, written by the celebrated Donna Marina di Escobar, who juridically declared that the servant of God, then dead, appeared to her at a time when she was suffering from dreadful pain in her chest, with such a burning fever, that she seemed to have, as it were, a fire within her. He looked at her with extreme benevolence, and said, "When we in heaven see those on earth suffer great pain and affliction, we often refrain from praying for them, in order not to deprive them of the opportunity of exercising virtue, and of meriting a greater recompense hereafter. Nevertheless thou art now relieved." "And," continues Donna Marina, "as he said these words I was entirely freed from pain, and I have heard that many other persons have obtained, through the intercession of the venerable father, great blessings both for soul and body." For all of which may honor and glory be given to God, now and forever.

CHAPTER XXIV

Profitable maxims found amongst the writings of Father de Ponte.

S a conclusion to this work the reader will not be displeased to receive a few short sentences found in the father's own handwriting after his holy death, entitled, "Spiritual Admonitions drawn from Prayer and Meditation." They form a mine of perfection and heavenly wisdom.

1. Do for God what thou canst, and God will do for thee what thou canst not.
2. Be faithful in little things, and God will help thee to accomplish great ones.
3. Defer not to the future the accomplishment of thy good purposes, because if thou dost not do now whilst thou art able, thou wilt every day become less willing.

4. Take the sweet things of this world as bitter, and the bitter sweet; thus thou shalt enjoy peace.

5. Think of God, and God will think of thee.

6. Be generous to thy neighbor, and God will be generous to thee.

7. Give to God what He asks of thee, and He will give thee what thou askest of Him.

8. If thou wishest to do the will of God, why negligently perform a duty of obedience under pretext of passing on to something else, since thou hast in reality what thou seekest?

9. If thou art inwardly disturbed at what thou dost, it is a sign thou aimest at something for thyself.

10. In me is nothing, in God is all.

11. I am what I am not; God is what He is.

12. True love of God seeks rather to suffer here than to rejoice, and to drink the chalice of bitterness rather than that of sweetness.

13. Real love of God prefers His glory to its own.

14. True love seeks to love rather than know, and esteems obedience more than knowledge.

15. Study to do those things only which God

SPIRITUAL MAXIMS

wills, and to do them all; then thou shalt have accomplished His will.

16. True love of God rejoices more to give than to receive, and if it desires to receive, it is only that it may be able to give.

17. Study to accomplish the will of God with promptitude and purity, simply because it is His will, from no other motive than to please Him; and thus thou shalt have done it on earth as it is done in heaven.

18. Thou lovest God in proportion as thou hatest thyself.

19. He truly hates himself who shuns honor and comfort, and who seeks opprobrium and suffering,

20. Choose for the companions of thy life poverty, contempt, and pain, because these were the chosen companions of Jesus Christ.

21. Whatever occupations thou mayest have, endeavor to do each action with as much perfection, peace, and composure, as if thou hadst nothing else to do.

22. Mortify eagerness to finish one action in order to pass quickly to another, and also any and every immoderate desire, unless thou wishest thy work to be ill done.

23. Use greater diligence in the services thou

hast to render than in the favors thou hast to receive.

24. Anxiety to receive favors from God renders us unfit to receive them because it is a sign of little humility and a want of purity of intention. Affection in action becomes tepid from an immoderate desire to receive.

25. He who is truly humble reputes himself unworthy of every good, and deserving of every evil, unworthy of favors, and deserving of chastisements.

26. If thou truly believest that thou deservest to dwell in hell, thou wilt neither complain of the evils thou sufferest nor of the blessings which thou hast not.

27. What hast thou given to God, or what hast thou done for Him, that thou shouldst dare to complain when He does not give thee what thou wishest?

28. If thou desirest always to think of God, study to forget thyself.

29. God will think of thee if thou forgettest thyself.

30. To forget oneself is to be unmindful of honors, conveniences, health, life, consolations, spiritual delights, and whatever concerns one's own interest, except inasmuch as God wills us to

remember them for His service and for His own greater glory.

31. Give more study to mortification than to contemplation, because an immortified person seeks the spirit of prayer, but cannot find it, whilst prayer itself seeks him who is truly mortified, and knows how to find him.

32. Experience teaches that a servile fear is often the punishment of the proud.

33. By a just judgment of God he who vainly and without reason glories in himself, fears needlessly and without reason.

34. He is near to evil who through sloth seeks the lesser good.

35. He is remote from evil who seeks the greater good.

36. God discloses Himself to him who humbly hides himself.

37. God conceals Himself from him who vainly displays himself.

38. That tongue is earthly which speaks well of self, ill of others, and never of God.

39. That tongue is heavenly which speaks ill of self, well of others, and always of God or for God.

40. Leave a letter begun when God calls thee,

because it is better to leave a letter well begun than badly finished.

41. God rearranges when obedience deranges thy ideas and the action thou art about.

42. It is the highest misery to be rich in conceit and poor in love, rich in learning and poor in virtue.

43. Vile man, set thy house in order, for tomorrow thou must die.

44. We act as God does when we do good, with peace and without perturbation; with love, without self-interest; with magnanimity, without presumption.

45. Thou wicked servant, take care what thou art about, for tomorrow thou shalt give an account of thy stewardship.

The End

www.ingramcontent.com/pod-product-compliance
Lightning Source LLC
Chambersburg PA
CBHW021441070526
44577CB00002B/246